LUXURY HOTELS
GOLF RESORTS

edited by Martin Nicholas Kunz & Patricia Massó

Texts written by Angelika Lerche

teNeues

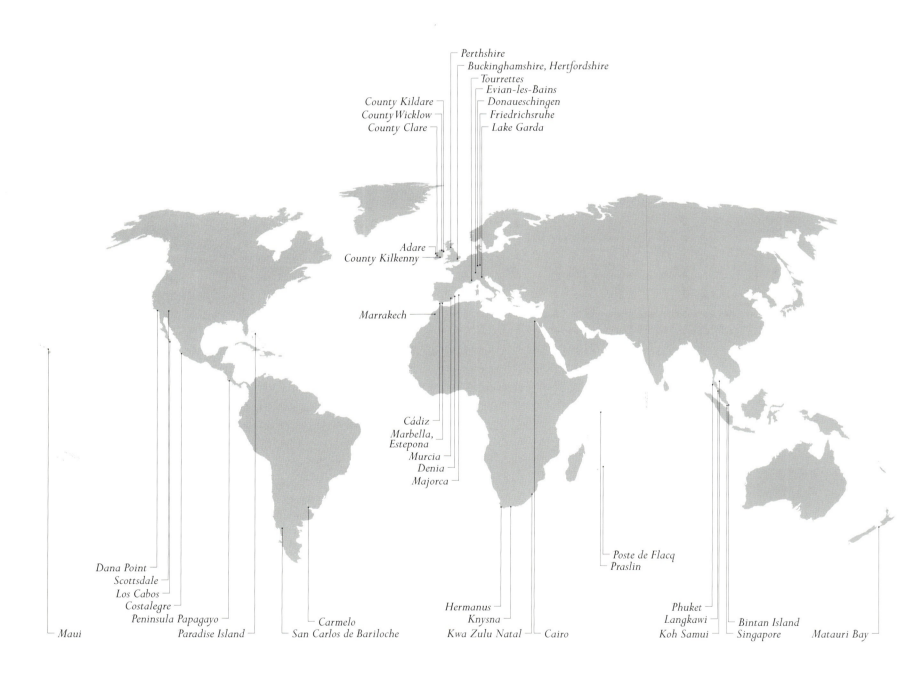

Luxury Hotels
GOLF RESORTS

	Introduction	4

Hawaii
Maui	Four Seasons Resort Maui at Wailea	14

California
Dana Point	St. Regis Resort, Monarch Beach	18

Arizona
Scottsdale	Four Seasons Resort Scottsdale at Troon North	24

Bahamas
Paradise Island	One&Only Ocean Club	30

Mexico
Costalegre	El Tamarindo	36
Los Cabos	One&Only Palmilla	42

Costa Rica
Peninsula Papagayo	Four Seasons Resort Costa Rica at Peninsula Papagayo	46

Argentina
San Carlos de Bariloche	Llao Llao Resort	50

Uruguay
Carmelo	Four Seasons Resort Carmelo	54

Scotland
Perthshire	The Gleneagles Hotel	58

England
Buckinghamshire	Stoke Park Club	62
Hertfordshire	The Grove	66

Ireland
County Wicklow	Marriott Druids Glen Hotel & Country Club	72
Adare	Adare Manor Hotel & Golf Resort	76
County Clare	Dromoland Castle	80
County Kildare	The K Club Golf Resort	84
County Kilkenny	Mount Juliet Conrad	90

Germany
Donaueschingen	Der Öschberghof	96
Friedrichsruhe	Schlosshotel Friedrichsruhe	100

Italy
Lake Garda	Palazzo Arzaga Hotel Spa & Golf Resort	104

France
Tourrettes	Four Seasons Resort Provence at Terre Blanche	108
Evian-les-Bains	Evian Royal Resort	112

Spain
Marbella	Rio Real Golf Hotel	116
Marbella	Villa Padierna	120
Estepona	Kempinski Hotel Bahía Estepona	124
Denia	Denia Marriott La Sella Golf Resort & Spa	128
Murcia	Hyatt Regency La Manga	132
Cádiz	San Roque Club	136
Majorca	ArabellaSheraton Golf Hotel Son Vida	142

Morocco
Marrakech	Amanjena	146

Egypt
Cairo	Oberoi Mena House	152

Mauritius
Poste de Flacq	Belle Mare Plage The Resort	156

Seychelles
Praslin	Lémuria Resort of Praslin	162

South Africa
Hermanus	The Western Cape Hotel & Spa	166
Kwa Zulu Natal	Zimbali Lodge	172
Knysna	Pezula Resort Hotel & Spa	176

Indonesia
Bintan Island	Banyan Tree Bintan	180

Malaysia
Langkawi	The Andaman	184
Langkawi	The Datai	188

Singapore
Singapore	The Sentosa Resort & Spa	192

Thailand
Phuket	Banyan Tree Phuket	196
Koh Samui	Bo Phut Resort & Spa	200
Koh Samui	Santiburi Resort	204

New Zealand
Matauri Bay	Kauri Cliffs Lodge	208

	Selected Courses	212
	Index	216
	Photo Credits	220

Links at the highest stage

Variety is the spice of life. That's also especially true for golfers. They constantly love to play on different courses, which they collect just like other people collect objets d'art. Somehow, the courses are a sort of collector's item: a gift of nature, finished by human hand.

Let's just think about spectacular desert golf courses. Here, lush, green fairways are winding their way over dusty sand, passing giant Saguaro cacti and quirky cliff formations. One of the most beautiful examples is the Pinnacle Course of Troon North in Arizona, located right next to the Four Seasons Resort Scottsdale. The traditional parkland courses are much older in design. They're magnificent facilities, often with old trees and they're the preferred tournament venues. But the British Open tournaments were first held on a links course in Scotland, the home of golf. In other words, the competition was on a course where some of the driving ranges run right along dramatic, beautiful coastlines or fabulous beaches. The word "link" in this case literally means the "link" between land and water. No matter whether it's a desert, parkland or on the coast: golf courses offer fascinating variety. Generally, a master of the sport had a hand in designing the most beautiful courses: with an extraordinary layout and always nestling in charming countryside. This makes them unique and distinctive.

If you start raving about such grand scenarios on the golf course, then you also want adequate accommodation—preferably so close to the fairways that you almost see golf balls flying by your window. Golf course managers and also hotel owners know that. That's why the same standard of hotel accompanies fantastic courses, or occasionally it's also the other way round. And just as the look of a golf course varies, the building style of hotel facilities also differs. At times, they're as ostentatious as an Italian palazzo, or they're as exotic as a village of huts in the rain forest; occasionally, they're designed in the style of Mexican casitas. But they always have one thing in common: they're luxurious, being created for people who share a love of high-quality and individual design. They're equipped with architecture that reflects the respective style of the region, conforming to the environment and enriching the country's culture, just like magnificent churches and castles; and their interior design fuels the imagination, while at the same time promising relaxation and leisure. Today, we need those things more than ever, to escape the stress of everyday life.

Luxury hotels are pleasant surroundings, where we like to spend time—somewhere we can be looked after and pampered to the highest possible standard. They're a rendezvous for like-minded individuals to meet up on a global scale; and they offer fascination and variety, while seducing us to visit special places. They also bring us just that little bit closer to our dreams. That's exactly what this book is about. This guide is luxuriously illustrated and includes short, descriptive texts that introduce you to the most beautiful golfing hotels in the world.

Angelika Lerche

Plätze von höchstem Niveau

Abwechslung ist die Würze des Lebens. Auch und gerade für Golfer. Sie lieben es, immer wieder andere Plätze zu spielen, sammeln sie, wie andere Leute Kunstobjekte, und um solche handelt es sich in gewisser Weise auch: Ein Geschenk der Natur, von Menschen vollendet.

Denken wir nur an die spektakulären Wüstenplätze. Da schlängeln sich saftig grüne Fairways über staubigen Sand, vorbei an riesigen Saguaro-Kakteen und skurrilen Felsformationen. Eines der schönsten Beispiele ist der Pinnacle Course von Troon North in Arizona, direkt neben dem Four Seasons Resort Scottsdale gelegen. Weitaus älter im Design sind die traditionellen Parklandkurse. Herrlich angelegt, oft mit altem Baumbestand, werden sie als Turnierplätze bevorzugt. Die British Open allerdings wurden zum ersten Mal auf einem Linkskurs in Schottland ausgetragen, der Wiege des Golfsports, also auf einem Platz, auf dem einige der Spielbahnen entlang dramatisch schöner Küsten oder herrlicher Strände verlaufen. Denn mit „Link" ist in diesem Zusammenhang die „Verbindung" zwischen Land und Wasser gemeint. Doch ob Wüste, Parkland oder Küste: Golfplätze bieten eine faszinierende Vielfalt. Die schönsten wurden von Meisterhand entworfen: mit außergewöhnlichem Layout und stets eingebettet in eine reizvolle Landschaft. Das macht sie einzigartig und unverwechselbar.

Kommt man angesichts solch grandioser Szenerien auf dem Golfplatz ins Schwelgen, will man adäquat wohnen, und am liebsten so dicht an den Fairways, dass man gewissermaßen die Golfbälle am Fenster vorbeifliegen sieht. Das wissen die Golfplatzbetreiber und das wissen auch die Hotelbesitzer. Daher gesellen sich zu großartigen Kursen ebensolche Hotels oder manchmal auch umgekehrt. Und so unterschiedlich wie das Aussehen der Golfplätze, so abwechslungsreich sind die Hotelanlagen in ihrer Bauweise. Mal sind sie prunkvoll wie ein italienischer Palazzo, mal exotisch wie ein Hüttendorf im Urwald, mal im Stil mexikanischer Casitas gestaltet. Eines aber ist ihnen immer gemeinsam: Sie sind luxuriös und geschaffen für Menschen, die die Liebe zu anspruchsvollem und individuellem Design teilen. Ausgestattet mit einer Architektur, die den jeweiligen Stil der Region widerspiegelt, sich dem Umfeld anpasst und die Kultur eines Landes bereichert, so wie prächtige Kirchen und Schlösser, und mit einem Interieur, das die Fantasie beflügelt und gleichzeitig Entspannung und Muße verspricht. Dinge, die wir heute mehr denn je brauchen, um dem Stress des Alltags zu entfliehen.

Luxushotels sind eine schöne Hülle, in der wir gerne verweilen, wo wir auf allerhöchstem Niveau umsorgt und verwöhnt werden. Sie sind Treffpunkt globaler Begegnungen für Menschen mit gleicher Wellenlänge, bieten Faszination und Abwechslung, entführen an besondere Orte und bringen uns unseren Träumen ein Stück näher. Genau darum geht es im vorliegenden Buch, das, üppig illustriert und mit kurzen beschreibenden Texten, zu den schönsten Golfhotels der Welt entführt.

Angelika Lerche

Des endroits du niveau élevé

La diversité est le sel de l'existence. Aussi et surtout pour les golfeurs. Ils aiment jouer sans cesse de nouveaux golfs, ils les collectionnent comme d'autres les objets d'art. D'une certaine façon, ce sont des œuvres d'art : un cadeau de la nature achevé par l'homme.

Il suffit de penser aux spectaculaires golfs dans le désert. Des fairways verdoyants serpentent sur du sable poussiéreux, côtoyant des cactus saguaro géants et des formations rocheuses bizarres. L'un des plus beaux exemples est le Pinnacle Course de Troon North en Arizona, situé directement à côté du Four Seasons Resort Scottsdale. Les traditionnels parcours de type parkland sont de conception beaucoup plus ancienne. Placés dans des cadres magnifiques, souvent boisés de vieux arbres, ils accueillent plutôt les compétitions. Le British Open toutefois a été disputé pour la première fois sur un links en Ecosse, berceau du golf. Un terrain donc où quelques-uns des fairways longent des côtes à la beauté sauvage ou de superbes plages. Dans ce cas, « links » suggère le lien entre la terre et l'eau. Les golfs, que ce soit des parklands, dans le désert ou sur la côte, offrent une incroyable diversité. Les plus beaux ont été créés par des maîtres en la matière : avec des tracés exceptionnels et toujours nichés dans de merveilleux paysages, ce qui les rend uniques et incomparables.

Etant donné des scénarios aussi grandioses et enthousiasmants sur le terrain de golf, un hébergement adéquat s'impose, le plus près possible des fairways, de façon à voir passer les balles en quelque sorte juste devant sa fenêtre. Les gérants de golfs et les propriétaires d'hôtel le savent. Aussi des hôtels formidables s'associent-ils à des golfs tout aussi formidables et parfois inversement. Et, de même que les golfs ont tous un aspect différent, de même les établissements hôteliers ont tous leur propre style. Ils sont fastueux comme un palais italien, exotiques comme un village de huttes dans la forêt vierge ou semblables à des casitas mexicaines. Mais ils ont toujours un point commun : ils sont tous luxueux et créés pour les hommes qui partagent le même amour du design individuel et exigeant. Leur architecture reflète le style de la région, s'intègre dans l'environnement et enrichit la culture du pays, comme des églises ou des châteaux admirables et leur intérieur stimule l'imagination tout en apportant détente et inspiration. Des choses dont nous avons plus que jamais besoin pour échapper au stress du quotidien.

Les hôtels de luxe sont de belles enveloppes où nous nous arrêtons un moment, où nous sommes suprêmement gâtés et couverts d'attentions. Ils sont le lieu vers lequel convergent des individus qui sont sur la même longueur d'onde, ils suscitent la fascination, procurent diversion et évasion dans des endroits uniques et nous rapprochent de nos rêves. C'est le sujet de cet ouvrage superbement illustré avec de courtes descriptions qui nous emmène dans les plus beaux hôtels de golf du monde.

Angelika Lerche

Lugares con mucha clase

La diversidad es la salsa de la vida. Más aún para los amantes del golf, que gozan jugando en lugares diferentes y coleccionándolos como quienes coleccionan objetos de arte; y en cierto modo es lo que son: un regalo de la naturaleza perfeccionado por el hombre.

Echemos una mirada a los espectaculares campos de golf en el desierto. Aquí los verdes y densos Fairways serpentean entre arena polvorienta, gigantescos cactus saguaro y grotescas formaciones rocosas. Uno de los ejemplos más bellos es el Pinnacle Course de Troon North en Arizona, situado directamente junto al Four Seasons Resort Scottsdale. En una línea de diseño más antigua tenemos los tradicionales recorridos en parque. Sus fantásticas ubicaciones, generalmente con arboledas primitivas, hacen de estos campos los favoritos para torneos. Sin embargo, los British Open tuvieron lugar por primera vez en un Link de Escocia, la cuna del golf, es decir, en un campo en el que algunas áreas de juego transcurren a lo largo de dramáticas costas o fabulosas playas. En este contexto el "Link" es claramente el "enlace" entre la tierra y el mar. Pero ya se trate de desierto, parque o costa, sin duda los campos de golf ofrecen una diversidad fascinante. Los más bellos fueron obra de maestros, con diseños excepcionales insertados en paisajes cautivadores. Siempre únicos e inconfundibles.

Ante la fascinación que produce semejante grandioso escenario en el campo de golf, uno desearía por encima de todo alojarse con la misma grandiosidad y a poder ser tan cerca de los Fairways que se vean pasar las bolas por la ventana. Tanto los gestores de campos de golf como los propietarios de hotel son conscientes de ello. De ahí que junto a tales magníficos campos se ubiquen magníficos hoteles, o viceversa. Y tan diversos son los campos de golf como lo es la arquitectura de los hoteles. Unas veces se levantan imponentes como un palazzo italiano, otras con el exotismo de un complejo de cabañas en la selva tropical, o bien como casitas en un pueblo mejicano. Pero todos cuentan con un denominador común: son lujosos y están concebidos para quienes comparten la pasión por el diseño exclusivo e individualista. Todos dotados de una arquitectura que refleja el estilo de cada región, que se adapta al entorno, y enriquece la cultura de un país, como hacen las espléndidas iglesias y castillos. Con interiores que dan rienda suelta a la imaginación y relajan e inspiran a la vez; necesidades éstas primordiales hoy más que nunca para liberarnos del estrés del día a día.

Los hoteles de lujo constituyen un hermoso paraguas que nos cubre, agasaja y cuida al más alto nivel. Son el punto de encuentro global para gente que vive en la misma onda. Ofrecen diversidad y producen fascinación: nos trasladan a lugares exclusivos y acercan a los sueños. Y este es el objetivo de una obra que con sus fantásticas ilustraciones y breves textos nos guía por los hoteles de golf más bellos del planeta.

Angelika Lerche

Luoghi con livello elevato

La varietà è il sale della vita. Anche e soprattutto per chi pratica il golf, che ama giocare su campi sempre diversi, collezionandoli, così come altri collezionano oggetti d'arte. E, in un certo senso, si tratta proprio di oggetti d'arte: un regalo della natura, perfezionato dall'uomo.

Basta pensare agli spettacolari campi da golf nel deserto, dove verdissimi fairway si snodano tra la sabbia polverosa, accanto a giganteschi cactus Saguaro e a bizzarre formazioni rocciose. Uno degli esempi più belli è il Pinnacle Course di Troon North in Arizona, in prossimità del Four Seasons Resort Scottsdale. Di design molto più tradizionale sono invece i percorsi realizzati nei parchi. In splendida posizione, spesso circondati da alberi secolari, sono i preferiti per i tornei. I British Open, tuttavia, sono stati disputati la prima volta su un link in Scozia, la culla del golf, e quindi su un campo in cui alcune delle piste corrono lungo coste di straordinaria bellezza o lungo magnifiche spiagge. In questo contesto, il termine "link" indica infatti il "collegamento" tra la terra e l'acqua. Insomma, che si trovino nel deserto, in un parco o sulla costa, la varietà offerta dai campi da golf è affascinante. I più belli sono stati disegnati da professionisti che ne hanno fatto dei capolavori: dal layout esclusivo, sempre incorniciati da uno stupendo paesaggio che li rende unici ed inconfondibili.

Dopo aver ammirato sul campo da golf lo splendore di questi scenari, nasce il desiderio di abitare in un posto altrettanto magnifico, possibilmente tanto vicino ai fairway da poter vedere – in un certo senso – le palline volare affacciandosi alla finestra. Ciò è risaputo sia dai gestori dei campi da golf sia dai proprietari degli hotel: essi uniscono quindi le loro risorse e mettono a disposizione dei propri ospiti percorsi e hotel di grande prestigio. A seconda dell'aspetto dei campi da golf, anche gli alberghi si differenziano nel loro stile architettonico. A volte sono sontuosi come un palazzo italiano, a volte esotici come un villaggio di capanne nella foresta vergine, altre ancora ricordano lo stile delle casitas messicane. Una cosa però hanno sempre in comune: il lusso, l'essere stati creati per coloro che condividono il piacere per lo stile esclusivo ed individuale. Arredati con elementi che rispecchiano lo stile del luogo in cui sorgono, sono in perfetta sintonia con l'ambiente e arricchiscono il patrimonio culturale del paese, come splendide chiese o castelli i cui interni stimolano la fantasia e promettono, allo stesso tempo, distensione e tranquillità. Cose di cui, oggi più che mai, abbiamo bisogno, per sfuggire allo stress a cui ci espone la vita di ogni giorno.

Gli hotel di lusso sono un bellissimo involucro in cui amiamo sostare, circondati di attenzioni e viziati da un servizio di prim'ordine. Sono un punto d'incontro per persone con la stessa lunghezza d'onda: essi ci seducono con il loro fascino e la varietà di stile e ci rapiscono in luoghi straordinari, avvicinandoci ai nostri sogni. E proprio questo è l'intento di questo libro, riccamente illustrato e corredato da brevi testi descrittivi: accompagnarci nei resort golfistici più belli del mondo.

Angelika Lerche

Four Seasons Resort Maui at Wailea
Maui, Hawaii

What makes you most enthusiastic? A crescent-shaped beach, with surfers riding the breaking waves and whales swimming about? Or the three championship golf courses right on your doorstep? This question should be cleared up before you move into one of the spacious suites, which either guarantees a view over the Pacific, the lush fairways or the fantastic garden facility with the breathtaking backdrop of the Haleakala volcano on the horizon. After this difficult decision, you'll find relaxation with a Hawaiian massage and dinner in the hotel's Spago restaurant.

Wofür begeistert man sich mehr? Den sichelförmigen Strand, an dem sich Wellen brechen, in denen Surfer reiten und Wale schwimmen? Oder die drei Championship-Golfplätze vor der Tür? Die Frage sollte geklärt sein, bevor man eine der großzügigen Suiten bezieht, die entweder Ausblick gewähren auf den Pazifik, die saftigen Fairways oder auf die herrliche Gartenanlage mit der atemberaubenden Kulisse des Vulkans Haleakala am Horizont. Nach dieser schwierigen Entscheidung findet man Erholung bei einer hawaiianischen Massage und einem Dinner im Hotelrestaurant Spago.

Qu'est-ce qui est le plus enthousiasmant ? La plage en forme de croissant sur laquelle viennent se briser les vagues où surfent les sportifs et où nagent les baleines ? Ou les trois parcours de championnat s'étendant face à l'hôtel ? Mieux vaut le savoir avant de s'installer dans l'une des immenses suites dont la vue donne ou sur l'océan ou sur les fairways verdoyants ou sur les magnifiques jardins avec l'impressionnant volcan Haleakala en coulisse à l'horizon. Après une décision si difficile vient la détente avec un massage hawaiien et un dîner au restaurant Spago de l'hôtel.

¿Qué será más fascinante? ¿La playa en forma de hoz con las desafiantes olas en las que cabalgan surfistas y nadan ballenas? ¿O más bien tener los tres campos de golf de torneo delante de la puerta? Cuestión a aclarar antes de ocupar una de las amplias suites, ya sea con vistas al Pacífico, a los pulidos Fairways o a unos jardines encantadores con el imponente volcán Haleakala como telón de fondo. Una vez tomada la difícil decisión se puede pasar al merecido descanso con masaje hawaiano y cena en el restaurante del hotel, el Spago.

Entusiasmarsi di più per la spiaggia a forma di falce dove si infrangono onde su cui si rincorrono i surfisti e nuotano le balene, o per i campi da golf da campionato a due passi dall'hotel? Sarà bene decidersi prima di occupare una delle spaziose suite con vista sul Pacifico, sui fairway lussureggianti o sugli splendidi giardini che, con il vulcano Haleakala stagliato all'orizzonte, offrono una vista di incomparabile bellezza. Dopo aver preso questa difficile decisione, ci si può riposare concedendosi un massaggio hawaiano o cenando al ristorante Spago, all'interno dell'hotel.

Despite the *considerable size of the hotel's estate, with 377 guest rooms including 75 suites, you'll find relaxation and tranquility here. The tropical natural landscape also helps you unwind.*

Trotz der *beachtlichen Größe der Anlage mit 377 Gästezimmern – darunter 75 Suiten – findet man hier erholsame Ruhe. Zur Entspannung trägt auch die tropische Naturlandschaft bei.*

Malgré les *dimensions impressionnantes du complexe – il compte 377 chambres dont 75 suites – on y trouve un calme apaisant. Le paysage tropical contribue à la détente.*

Si bien *se trata de un complejo de grandes dimensiones, con 377 habitaciones, de las cuales 75 son suites, la tranquilidad y el relax están garantizados. Sin duda el paisaje tropical también contribuye a ello.*

Nonostante le *considerevoli dimensioni della struttura, che dispone di 377 camere, tra le quali 75 suite, l'hotel assicura un soggiorno tranquillo e rilassante, nella cornice di un paesaggio immerso nella natura tropicale.*

Here, exclusivity dominates everywhere: in the suites, on the fabulous terraces and by the pool.
Exklusivität herrscht hier allerorten: in den Suiten, auf den herrlichen Terrassen und am Pool.
L'exclusivité est omniprésente : dans les suites, sur les magnifiques terrasses et au bord de la piscine.
La exclusividad siempre presente: en las suites, las magníficas terrazas y la piscina.
Qui l'esclusività regna ovunque: nelle suite, sulle magnifiche terrazze e nei pressi della piscina.

Four Seasons Resort Maui at Wailea *Maui, Hawaii*

St. Regis Resort, Monarch Beach
Dana Point, California

The St. Regis Resort, Monarch Beach is presented high above the Pacific coastline, south of Los Angeles. With its white stucco walls, columns and magnificent fountains, it's like a Mediterranean palace. Your eye roams freely across miles of sandy beaches—they count amongst the most beautiful in California. The extensive resort is equipped with every imaginable comfort. A world-class spa and private beach club are all-inclusive. Golfers meet their challenge on the Monarch Beach Golf Links, a masterpiece by Robert Trent Jones Jr.

Wie ein mediterraner Palast, mit weißen Stuckmauern, Säulen und prachtvollen Brunnen, präsentiert sich das St. Regis Resort, Monarch Beach, hoch über der Küste des Pazifischen Ozeans, südlich von Los Angeles. Frei schweift der Blick über kilometerlange Sandstrände – die zu den schönsten in Kalifornien zählen. Ausgestattet ist die weitläufige Anlage mit allem erdenklichen Komfort. Weltklasse-Spa und privater Beach-Club sind inklusive. Golfer finden ihre Herausforderung auf dem Monarch Beach Golf Links, einem Meisterstück von Robert Trent Jones Jr.

Tel un palais méditerranéen aux murs en stuc blanc, avec des colonnes et de superbes fontaines, le St. Regis Resort, Monarch Beach se dresse au-dessus de la côte du Pacifique au sud de Los Angeles. Le regard se perd sur des kilomètres de plages de sable qui comptent parmi les plus belles de Californie. Ce domaine très étendu est doté de tout le confort possible, avec bien entendu un spa de grande classe et un bar beach-club privé. Quant aux golfeurs, le défi a pour nom Monarch Beach Golf Links Course, un chef d'œuvre de Robert Trent Jones Jr.

Al sur de Los Angeles, en la costa del Océano Pacífico se levanta el St. Regis Resort, Monarch Beach concebido como un palacio de estilo mediterráneo con sus paredes blancas, columnatas e imponentes fuentes. Desde lo alto la vista abarca quilométricas playas que se consideran entre las más bellas de California. El amplio complejo hotelero es todo un derroche de confort que incluye un Spa de alta categoría y un Beach-Club privado. Para los amantes del golf el reto lo propone el Monarch Beach Golf Links Course, un recorrido magistralmente diseñado por Robert Trent Jones Jr.

Come un palazzo di stile mediterraneo, dai muri bianchi e stuccati, impreziosito da colonne e da imponenti fontane, si presenta il St. Regis Resort, Monarch Beach arroccato sulla costa dell'Oceano Pacifico, a sud di Los Angeles. Lo sguardo scivola libero su lunghissime spiagge sabbiose, tra le più belle della California. La vasta struttura è dotata di ogni tipo di comfort. Spa di altissimo livello e beach club privato sono inclusi. Gli appassionati di golf avranno occasione di giocare sul Monarch Beach Golf Links Course, un capolavoro di Robert Trent Jones Jr.

The atmosphere *by the pool in the spa is intimate, in contrast to the open expanse of the golf course and the Pacific beaches.*

Die Atmosphäre *am Pool des Spas ist intim, im Gegensatz zur offenen Weite des Golfplatzes und der Pazifikstrände.*

Les bords *de la piscine du spa sont un endroit intime au contraire des étendues du terrain de golf et des plages du Pacifique.*

La piscina *del Spa emana un ambiente íntimo, en contrapartida con la magnitud del campo de golf y las playas del Pacífico.*

L'atmosfera che *regna sulla piscina della Spa è intima, in contrasto con la spaziosità del campo da golf e delle spiagge del Pacifico.*

The furnishing is varied, with styles alternating from the magnificent lobby to the art déco bistro and contemporary designed guest rooms and suites.

Die Ausstattung ist vielfältig, die Stile wechseln von der prunkvollen Lobby über das Art Deco Bistro bis hin zu den zeitgenössisch gestalteten Gästezimmern und Suiten.

Les équipements sont multiples, les styles varient, allant du fastueux lobby au bistro Art Déco jusqu'aux chambres et suites à l'aménagement contemporain.

La decoración de los interiores es diversa, con estilos que van desde el carácter majestuoso del hall, pasando por el Art Deco del bistró, hasta los diseños contemporáneos de las habitaciones y suites.

L'arredamento è vario. Gli stili si alternano passando dalla sontuosa lobby all'Art Deco bistro fino alle camere e alle suite in stile moderno.

St. Regis Resort, Monarch Beach *Dana Point, California*

Four Seasons Resort Scottsdale at Troon North

Scottsdale, Arizona

Surrounded by the Sonora desert and the stony foothills of Pinnacle Peak, the 25 "Casitas", with simple architecture, are grouped around a main building and make the resort look like a Mexican village. The 210 rooms and suites are luxuriously furnished, offering a refreshing pool on a private terrace and a clear view of bizarre cliff formations and giant Saguaro cacti. Amidst this ambiance, you're invited to play on one of Arizona's most spectacular golf courses. Afterwards, you may enjoy an authentic hot stone therapy and the excellent Mexican-style cuisine.

Umgeben von der Sonora Wüste und den steinigen Ausläufern des Pinnacle Peak, gruppieren sich 25 „Casitas" in schlichter Architektur um ein Haupthaus und lassen das Resort wie ein mexikanisches Dorf erscheinen. Die 210 Zimmer und Suiten sind luxuriös ausgestattet, bieten einen Erfrischungspool auf eigener Terrasse und einen freien Blick auf bizarre Felsformationen und riesige Saguaro-Kakteen. Mitten in diesem Ambiente lädt einer der spektakulärsten Golfplätze Arizonas zum Spiel ein. Danach genießt man eine authentische Hot Stone Therapie und die exzellente Küche mexikanischer Art.

Entourées par le désert de Sonora et les contreforts rocailleux du Pinnacle Peak, 25 « casitas » à l'architecture sobre se groupent autour du bâtiment principal, le tout ressemblant à un village mexicain. Les 210 chambres et suites sont luxueusement équipées, avec piscine rafraîchissante sur une terrasse privée et panorama sur les bizarres formations rocheuses et les cactus saguaro géants. C'est dans ce cadre que se situe l'un des plus spectaculaires terrains de golf d'Arizona. Le golfeur profite ensuite d'une authentique hot stone thérapie et savoure l'excellente cuisine aux saveurs mexicaines.

El desierto de Sonora y las estribaciones rocosas del Pinnacle Peak envuelven a estas 25 "Casitas" de arquitectura austera agrupadas en torno a un edificio principal. Un resort que bien podría ser cualquier pueblecito mejicano. Las 210 habitaciones y suites tienen equipamiento de lujo y cuentan con piscina y terraza propias, además de amplias vistas a las singulares formaciones rocosas y a los gigantescos cactus saguaro. En semejante entorno invita al juego uno de los campos de golf más espectaculares de Arizona. El placer continúa disfrutando de un auténtico masaje con piedras calientes y de la excelente cocina mejicana.

Circondate dal deserto di Sonora e dalle propaggini sassose del Pinnacle Peak, 25 "casitas" dall'architettura sobria si raggruppano intorno ad un edificio principale, conferendo alla struttura l'aspetto di un villaggio messicano. Le 210 camere e suite sono lussuosamente arredate, dispongono di terrazza propria con piscina rinfrescante da cui si possono ammirare le bizzarre formazioni rocciose ed i giganteschi cactus Saguaro. Nel mezzo di questa atmosfera, uno dei campi da golf più spettacolari dell'Arizona invita al gioco, al termine del quale sarà possibile rilassarsi con un'autentica terapia hot stone e gustare l'eccellente cucina di tipo messicano.

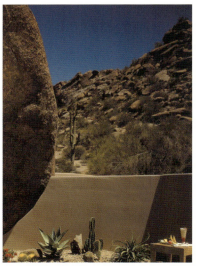

Desert golf means target golf. The Pinnacle Course of Troon North is one of the most beautiful examples.

Wüstengolf bedeutet „Target-Golf". Der Pinnacle Course von Troon North ist eines der schönsten Beispiele.

Le golf dans le désert est synonyme de « target-golf ». La Pinnacle Course de Troon North en est l'un des plus beaux exemples.

Golf en el desierto es sinónimo de "target golf". El Pinnacle Course de Troon North es uno de los ejemplos más bellos.

Golf nel deserto significa target golf. Il Pinnacle Course di Troon North ne è uno degli esempi più belli.

The pools are refreshing on hot afternoons. Open fires in the hearth take care of comfort when the cool nights draw in.

Pools erfrischen an heißen Nachmittagen. Kaminfeuer sorgen für Behaglichkeit, wenn die kühlen Nächte hereinbrechen.

Pour la chaleur de l'après-midi, c'est la piscine qui rafraîchit. Le feu de cheminée crée une sensation de bien-être quand la fraîcheur de la nuit se répand.

Las piscinas sirven de alivio en tardes calurosas y el calor de la chimenea templa y hace entrañables las noches frescas.

Le piscine permettono di rinfrescarsi nei caldi pomeriggi. Il fuoco del camino crea una piacevole intimità nelle notti fresche.

One&Only Ocean Club
Paradise Island, Bahamas

The name already says it: paradise is right here. It's directly opposite the busy Nassau harbor, between wide beaches and terrace-shaped gardens that are reminiscent of Versailles. At the gardens' highest point, the arches of a 14th century gateway from an Augustinian monastery are still standing. From here, you have a sweeping view of the club's entire estate, with 106 rooms and suites in several colonial-style buildings, in cottages and villas. And just like in paradise, every day you're tempted with fresh fruits—and of course, Champagne as well.

Der Name sagt es schon: Hier liegt das Paradies. Gleich gegenüber dem quirligen Nassauer Hafen, zwischen weiten Stränden und terrassenförmigen Gärten, die an Versailles erinnern. An deren höchster Stelle stehen die Torbögen eines Augustinerklosters aus dem 14. Jahrhundert. Von dort schweift der Blick über die gesamte Clubanlage, deren 106 Zimmer und Suiten über mehrere Gebäude im Kolonialstil, in Cottages und Villen verteilt sind. Und wie im Paradies, wird man täglich mit frischen Früchten verführt und natürlich gibt es dazu Champagner.

Comme son nom l'indique, c'est le paradis. Situé à l'opposé du port animé de Nassau, entre d'immenses plages et des jardins en terrasses inspirés par Versailles. L'hôtel est dominé par les arcades d'un cloître augustin du 14ème siècle. De là s'offre une vue panoramique sur l'ensemble du club dont les 106 chambres et suites sont réparties sur plusieurs bâtiments au style colonial, des cottages et des villas. Et comme au paradis il y a tous les jours profusion de fruits frais – arrosés de champagne bien entendu.

Sin duda el paraíso, como su nombre indica. Y ubicado justo enfrente del ajetreado puerto de Nassau, entre vastas playas y jardines dispuestos en terraza que recuerdan a Versalles. En su punto más elevado se levantan las arcadas de un monasterio agustino del siglo XIV. Desde allí la vista abarca todo el recinto del club, con 106 habitaciones y suites repartidas entre varios edificios tipo casitas y villas de estilo colonial. Y como suele ocurrir en el paraíso, uno se deja seducir a diario con frutas frescas… acompañadas de champán.

Lo dice il nome: questo è il paradiso. La struttura si trova proprio di fronte al vivace porto di Nassau, tra ampie spiagge e giardini a terrazza che ricordano quelli di Versailles, alla cui cima si stagliano gli archi del portale di un convento agostiniano del 14° secolo. Da lì lo sguardo si perde sull'intera struttura del club, le cui 106 camere e suite sono suddivise in edifici di stile coloniale, cottage e ville. E, come nel paradiso, tutti i giorni si è tentati da ogni varietà di frutta fresca accompagnata – naturalmente – da champagne.

The color white corresponds over and over again to the blue of the ocean—at breakfast, in the spa, on the terraces.

Immer wieder korrespondiert die Farbe Weiß mit dem Blau des Ozeans: beim Frühstück, im Spa, auf den Terrassen.

Ici le blanc répond toujours au bleu de l'océan : au petit déjeuner, dans le spa, sur les terrasses.

En el desayuno, en el Spa o en la terraza se contempla sin fin un blanco que armoniza con el azul del océano.

Il colore bianco si alterna continuamente all'azzurro dell'oceano: a colazione, nella spa, sulle terrazze.

Living with a view of Tom Weiskopf's design of the PGA golf course and the Atlantic.
Wohnen mit Blick auf den von Tom Weiskopf konzipierten PGA-Golfplatz und den Atlantik.
Une résidence avec vue sur le parcours PGA dessiné par Tom Weiskopf et sur l'Atlantique.
Alojarse con vistas al Atlántico y al campo de Golf de la PGA concebido por Tom Weiskopf.
Abitare con vista sul campo da golf PGA ideato da Tom Weiskopf e sull'Atlantico.

One&Only Ocean Club *Paradise Island, Bahamas*

No matter whether it's in drawings, on ornaments or in the courtyard of the world-class spa—there are lots of palm trees on Paradise Island.

Ob in Zeichnungen, Ornamenten oder im Hof des Weltklasse-Spa – Palmen gibt es viele auf Paradise Island.

Que ce soit sur des dessins, des décorations ou dans la cour du spa de très grande classe – il y a beaucoup de cocotiers sur Paradise Island.

El Paradise Island está salpicado de palmeras, ya sea en dibujos, ornamentos, o en el patio del exclusivo Spa.

Nei disegni, negli ornamenti e nel cortile di questa spa di gran classe – palme, palme e ancora palme a Paradise Island.

One&Only Ocean Club *Paradise Island, Bahamas*

El Tamarindo

Costalegre, Mexico

Live like Robinson Crusoe, only with much more luxury. 28 villas are located right on the Pacific coast and sheltered by giant tropical trees. The décor inside the villas is relaxing and restrained, in contrast to the lush nature that is the focal point here. Life is enjoyed mainly outdoors. Of course, this also means enjoying the championship golf course that stretches over the cliffs and dunes of two beaches and as far as the tropical forests. In the jungle spa, right beneath the palm trees, guests can enjoy various massages; in La Higuera restaurant, they sample the excellent cuisine beneath the shade of a fig tree and with a clear sea view.

Leben wie Robinson Crusoe, nur viel luxuriöser. 28 Villen liegen behütet von Urwaldriesen, direkt an der Pazifikküste. Ihre Ausstattung ist wohltuend zurückhaltend, im Kontrast zur üppigen Natur, die hier im Mittelpunkt steht. Das Leben spielt sich hauptsächlich draußen ab. Natürlich auch auf dem Championship-Golfplatz, der sich über die Klippen und Dünen von zwei Stränden bis zu den tropischen Wäldern erstreckt. Im Dschungel-Spa können Gäste diverse Massagen direkt unter den Palmen genießen, während im Restaurant La Higuera die exzellente Küche im Schatten eines Feigenbaumes mit freiem Blick aufs Meer lockt.

Vivre comme Robinson Crusoë, le luxe en plus. Les géants de la forêt vierge protègent 28 villas installées directement sur la côte du Pacifique. Leur aménagement d'une salutaire discrétion contraste avec l'exubérance de la nature, ici l'élément dominant. La vie se déroule essentiellement en plein air. Bien sûr aussi sur le parcours de championnat de golf qui s'étend au-delà des écueils et des dunes de deux plages jusqu'aux forêts tropicales. Dans le spa au cœur de la jungle les hôtes bénéficient de divers massages directement sous les palmiers et savourent dans le restaurant La Higuera une excellente cuisine à l'ombre d'un figuier avec vue sur la mer.

Es como la vida de Robinson Crusoe, pero a todo lujo. Se trata de 28 villas protegidas por la selva tropical justo a las puertas de la costa del Pacífico. La decoración relajante y sin excesos contrasta con la vegetación exuberante que domina un lugar concebido para disfrutar del exterior; y qué mejor opción para ello que el campo de golf de campeonato, que se prolonga sobre acantilados y dunas desde las dos playas hasta la selva tropical. El centro Spa en la selva ofrece a sus clientes la posibilidad de gozar de los diversos masajes bajo las palmeras. En el restaurante La Higuera el placer lo propone una excelente cocina y las vistas abiertas al mar, bajo el árbol que da nombre al local.

Vivere come Robinson Crusoe, ma in modo molto più lussuoso. 28 ville si trovano direttamente sulla costa dell'Oceano Pacifico, protette dai giganteschi alberi della foresta vergine. L'arredamento è piacevolmente sobrio, in contrasto con la natura rigogliosa che circonda ogni cosa. La vita si svolge soprattutto fuori. Naturalmente anche nel campo da golf da campionato che si stende sugli scogli e le dune di due spiagge fino alle foreste tropicali. Nella spa della giungla è possibile concedersi diversi massaggi direttamente sotto le palme, mentre nel ristorante La Higuera, con vista sul mare, si può gustare l'ottima cucina all'ombra degli alberi di fico.

You could jump directly into the sea or one of the pools from the golf course.

Vom Golfplatz aus könnte man direkt ins Meer oder einen der Pools springen.

Du golf on pourrait plonger directement dans la mer ou dans l'une des piscines.

Desde el campo de golf se podría saltar al mar o las piscinas directamente.

Dal campo di golf ci si potrebbe tuffare direttamente nel mare o in una delle piscine.

The simplicity of the rooms, their color scheme and the connection of the architecture with the surroundings offer relaxation for mind, body and soul. The game of golf also promotes this harmony.

Die Einfachheit der Räume, ihre Farbgebung und die Verbundenheit der Architektur mit der Umgebung bieten Entspannung für Geist, Seele und Körper. Eine Harmonie, die auch das Golfspiel fördert.

La simplicité des pièces, les coloris et l'harmonie de l'architecture avec l'environnement sont une détente pour l'esprit, l'âme et le corps. Une harmonie qui favorise l'adresse du jeu au golf.

La sencillez y el tono de las estancias, ligado a una arquitectura en consonancia con el entorno, proporcionan relax para cuerpo y alma. Una armonía que se acentúa a través del golf.

La semplicità degli spazi, il loro colore e la simbiosi tra architettura e ambiente, offrono relax per lo spirito, la mente e il corpo. Un'armonia che giova anche al gioco del golf.

El Tamarindo *Costalegre, Mexico*   39

The resort's secluded location and size—with only 28 villas on an area of 2100 acres—means you'll find the highest degree of privacy, as if you're all alone with the sky and sea.

Bei der Abgeschiedenheit und Größe des Resorts mit nur 28 Villen auf einer Fläche von 850 Hektar findet man Privatheit in höchstem Maß, als wäre man mit sich, dem Himmel und dem Meer allein.

Grâce à l'isolement et aux dimensions du resort ne comportant que 28 villas sur une surface de 850 hectares, il règne une extrême intimité, comme si l'on était seul avec le ciel et la mer.

El aislamiento y las dimensiones del resort, con tan sólo 28 villas repartidas en 850 hectáreas, prestan privacidad en extremo para encontrarse con sí mismo, el mar y el cielo.

L'isolamento e le dimensioni del resort, con soltanto 28 ville su una superficie di 850 ettari, garantiscono privacy assoluta, come se si fosse soli con se stessi, il cielo e il mare.

El Tamarindo *Costalegre, Mexico*

One&Only Palmilla

Los Cabos, Mexico

The Baja California in the north west of Mexico belongs to the most spectacular landscapes in the world. The One&Only Palmilla is located at its southern-most point, surrounded by desert and sea. With white chalk walls, red-tiled roofs, cool springs, lots of iron fretwork art and an historical wedding chapel, the resort reflects the gracious style of old Mexico. The new Mexico is represented by a high-quality spa, a fitness center and the restaurant "C", where haute cuisine is served, a creation of Charlie Trotter, one of America's top chefs.

Die Baja California im Nordwesten Mexikos gehört zu den spektakulärsten Landschaften der Welt. An ihrem südlichsten Punkt liegt das One&Only Palmilla, umgeben von Wüste und Meer. Mit weißen Kalkwänden, roten Ziegeldächern, kühlen Springbrunnen, viel schmiedeeiserner Kunst und einer historischen Hochzeitskapelle, reflektiert das Resort den graziösen Stil des alten Mexiko. Das neue Mexiko präsentiert sich mit einem hochwertigen Spa, einem Fitnesszentrum und dem Restaurant „C", in dem Haute Cuisine serviert wird, kreiert von Charlie Trotter, einem der Spitzenköche Amerikas.

L'Etat de Baja California au nord-ouest du Mexique possède les paysages les plus spectaculaires du monde. Le One&Only Palmilla se trouve à la pointe extrême sud, entre mer et désert. L'hôtel aux murs blanchis à la chaux, aux tuiles rouges, aux fontaines fraîches, aux nombreuses ferronneries d'art et près d'une chapelle historique pour la célébration de mariages rappelle l'architecture gracieuse du vieux Mexique. Le nouveau Mexique est représenté par un spa de grand luxe, un centre de fitness et le restaurant « C » qui sert de la haute cuisine créée par Charlie Trotter, l'un des chefs les plus talentueux d'Amérique.

La Baja California en el noroeste de México constituye uno de los paisajes más espectaculares del mundo. En su extremo sur y circundado por el mar y el desierto, se ubica el One&Only Palmilla. Sus paredes encaladas, tejados rojos, fuentes primorosas, trabajos de hierro forjado y una capilla histórica para bodas, visten al lugar del estilo pintoresco del viejo México. Pero para caracterizar al México de hoy, el resort cuenta con un excelente Spa, un gimnasio y el restaurante "C", en el que la alta cocina está presente de la mano de Charlie Trotter, gran cocinero americano.

La Baja California nel nord-ovest del Messico fa parte dei paesaggi più spettacolari del mondo. Al suo punto più meridionale si trova il One&Only Palmilla, circondato dal deserto e dal mare. Con le pareti imbiancate a calce, i tetti dalle tegole rosse, le fresche fontane a zampillo, ornamenti artistici in ferro battuto ed una storica cappella nuziale, il resort riflette il grazioso stile del vecchio Messico. Il nuovo Messico si presenta con una spa di gran classe, un centro di fitness ed il ristorante „C", in cui viene servita haute cuisine creata da Charlie Trotter, uno dei più grandi cuochi d'America.

With tall cacti, deep ravines and fabulous views of the Sea of Cortez, the 27-hole golf course by Jack Nicklaus counts amongst the best in the world.

Mit hohen Kakteen, tiefen Schluchten und herrlichen Aussichten auf die Sea of Cortez, zählt der 27-Loch-Golfplatz von Jack Nicklaus zu den besten der Welt.

Avec de hauts cactus, des gorges profondes et une vue spectaculaire sur la mer de Cortez, le parcours de 27 trous signé Jack Nicklaus est classé comme l'un des meilleurs au monde.

El campo de golf de 27 hoyos de Jack Nicklaus, uno de los mejores del mundo, se abre entre enormes cactus, cañones escarpados e imponentes vistas al Mar de Cortés.

Con alti cactus, gole profonde e magnifici scorci sul Mare di Cortez, il campo da golf a 27 buche di Jack Nicklaus si annovera tra i migliori del mondo.

A personal butler is part of the service in the 174 casually elegant rooms and suites and, depending on the time of year, a telescope for whale watching.

Zum Service der 174 leger-eleganten Zimmer und Suiten gehört ein persönlicher Butler und je nach Jahreszeit ein Teleskop zum Beobachten von Walen.

Chacune des 174 chambres et suites, à l'élégance légère, dispose d'un majordome personnel et, selon la saison, d'un télescope pour l'observation des baleines.

Las 174 habitaciones y suites de toque elegante y fresco, incluyen en el servicio un mayordomo y, dependiendo de la estación, un telescopio para observar las ballenas.

Del servizio delle 174 camere e suite, arredate in stile semplice ed elegante, fa parte un maggiordomo personale e, a seconda della stagione, un telescopio per osservare le balene.

Four Seasons Resort Costa Rica at Peninsula Papagayo

Peninsula Papagayo, Costa Rica

Rain forests in lavish green, with flora and fauna rich in all different species, volcanoes, waterfalls and hot springs are the backdrops for the resort, bordering on two magnificent beaches. A total of 165 rooms and suites, all with a private balcony or terrace, are designed in warm, strong colors that compliment the lush nature. The exquisite comfort is also visible in generously designed baths and extremely comfortable beds. A luxurious spa offers fitness practices that are inspired by the tropical location.

Regenwälder in sattem Grün, mit einer artenreichen Fauna und Flora, Vulkanen, Wasserfällen und heißen Quellen, sind Kulisse für das Resort, das an zwei herrliche Strände grenzt. Die insgesamt 165 Zimmer und Suiten, alle mit Balkon oder Terrasse, sind in warmen, kräftigen Farben gestaltet, passend zur üppigen Natur. Der exquisite Komfort zeigt sich auch in den großzügig angelegten Bädern und den außerordentlich bequemen Betten. Ein luxuriöses Spa bietet tropisch inspirierte Wellness-Anwendungen.

Le resort bordé de deux magnifiques plages a pour toile de fond des forêts tropicales au vert profond avec une faune et une flore très diversifiées, des volcans, des cascades et des sources chaudes. Les 165 chambres et suites comportant toutes un balcon ou une terrasse, sont de couleurs vives et chaudes assorties à la nature luxuriante. Le confort exquis se traduit entre autres dans les salles de bain spacieuses et les lits exceptionnellement confortables. Un luxueux spa propose des soins de bien-être d'inspiration tropicale.

Un escenario de selva exuberante, fauna y flora de gran diversidad, volcanes, cascadas y fuentes termales, encuadran a este resort que limita con dos maravillosas playas. Sus 165 habitaciones y suites cuentan todas con balcón o terraza y están decoradas con colores vivos y cálidos en plena armonía con la naturaleza. Muestras de un confort exquisito son los amplios baños y las camas extraordinariamente confortables. El lujoso Spa ofrece tratamientos Wellness inspirados en el trópico.

Foreste tropicali verdissime con una grande varietà di fauna e flora, vulcani, cascate e sorgenti calde fanno da sfondo al resort, delimitato da due splendide spiagge. Tutte le camere e le suite, 165 in totale, hanno balcone o terrazza, e sono arredate con colori caldi e forti, in armonia con la natura lussureggiante. Di squisito comfort sono anche i bagni spaziosi e i letti straordinariamente comodi. Una lussiosa spa mette a disposizione trattamenti di wellness ispirati all'ambiente tropicale.

The Arnold Palmer 14-hole golf course, opened in 2004, guarantees a fabulous view of the Pacific Ocean.

Der 2004 eröffnete Arnold Palmer Golfplatz gewährt an 14 Löchern eine herrliche Aussicht auf den Pazifischen Ozean.

Le golf dessiné par Arnold Palmer a ouvert en 2004 ; 14 de ses trous offrent des points de vue magnifiques sur le Pacifique.

El campo de golf, obra de Arnold Palmer e inaugurado en 2004, cuenta con 14 hoyos y un panorama precioso del Océano Pacífico.

Il campo da golf con 14 buche Arnold Palmer, aperto nel 2004, permette un'incantevole vista sull'Oceano Pacifico.

A real pleasure: dining outdoors, surrounded by three pools and fascinating nature.

Ein echter Genuss: Speisen unter freiem Himmel, umgeben von drei Pools und faszinierender Natur.

Un pur régal: un repas en plein air, entouré de trois piscines et d'une nature fascinante.

Un verdadero deleite: disfrutar de la comida a cielo abierto con tres piscinas y una naturaleza fascinante ente la vista.

Un vero lusso: la possibilità di cenare all'aperto, circondati da tre piscine e dallo splendore della natura.

Four Seasons Resort Costa Rica at Peninsula Papagayo *Peninsula Papagayo, Costa Rica*

Llao Llao Resort
San Carlos de Bariloche, Argentina

The best steaks come from Argentina. You'll see why when you look at the countryside. Nature is unspoilt and looks fresh; and it's especially beautiful between the Nahuel Huapi national park and Moreno Lake, with the majestic peaks of Mount López and Mount Tronador in the background. This is the ideal place for the Llao Llao Hotel, built by the architect Alejandro Bustillo in 1940. Meanwhile, the hotel has been restored and equipped with every modern comfort like a spa and health club. The hotel is a jewel of South American golf resorts.

Aus Argentinien kommen mit die besten Steaks. Wenn man die Landschaft betrachtet, weiß man warum. Die Natur ist unbelastet und wirkt frisch. Besonders schön ist sie zwischen dem Nationalpark Nahuel Huapi und dem Moreno See, mit den majestätischen Gipfeln von Mount López und Mount Tronador im Hintergrund. Der ideale Platz für das 1940 von Architekt Alejandro Bustillo erbaute Llao Llao Hotel. Inzwischen renoviert und mit allem modernen Komfort wie Spa und Health Club ausgestattet, ist es ein Juwel der südamerikanischen Golf Resorts.

Les steaks d'Argentine sont parmi les meilleurs. Quand on voit ses paysages on comprend pourquoi. Intacte, la nature a l'air fraîche. Elle est particulièrement belle entre le parc national Nahuel Huapi et le lac Moreno avec les sommets majestueux des Monts López et Tronador à l'arrière-plan. Un site idéal pour l'hôtel Llao Llao construit en 1940 par l'architecte Alejandro Bustillo. Entre-temps rénové et doté de tout le confort moderne, tel un spa et un health club, c'est un des joyaux des golf-resorts sud-américains.

El chuletón argentino, el mejor; basta con observar el paisaje para saber por qué. La naturaleza es pura, sana y está dotada de una belleza especialmente llamativa entre el parque national Nahuel Huapí y lagos Moreno, con los majestuosos picos López y Tronador como testigos. Un escenario ideal para el hotel Llao Llao, concebido en 1940 por el arquitecto Alejandro Bustillo. Posteriormente ha sido renovado y dotado con el más moderno confort que proponen su Spa y Health Club, convirtiéndose así en una verdadera joya dentro de los resorts de golf sudamericanos.

Dall'Argentina arrivano le migliori bistecche. Se si osserva il paesaggio, si capisce il perché: la natura è incontaminata e fresca, di bellezza particolare soprattutto tra il parco nationale Nahuel Huapi ed il lago Moreno, con le maestose vette del monte López e del monte Tronador sullo sfondo. Il posto ideale per l'hotel Llao Llao, costruito nel 1940 dall'architetto Alejandro Bustillo. Nel frattempo ristrutturato e dotato di tutti i moderni comfort, come spa e health club, questo hotel è un gioiello tra i resort golfistici del Sudamerica.

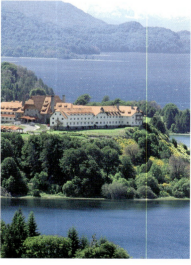

A golf course in Patagonia, with a landscape just like in Switzerland: mountains, forests and lakes.

Ein Golfplatz in Patagonien, mit einer Landschaft wie in der Schweiz: Berge, Wälder und Seen.

Un terrain de golf en Patagonie avec un paysage comme en Suisse : montagnes, forêts et lacs.

Un campo de golf en la Patagonia con un paisaje como el de Suiza: todo mar, bosque y lagos.

Un campo da golf in Patagonia ed un paesaggio come in Svizzera: montagne, boschi e laghi.

Tasteful interior in local style; floor-to-ceiling glass walls give an open vista of the enchanting mountain scenery.

Geschmackvolles Interieur im Landesstil; raumhohe Glaswände geben den Blick frei auf die traumhafte Kulisse der Berge.

Un intérieur décoré avec goût dans le style local, des cloisons de baies vitrées ouvrent le panorama sur la merveilleuse toile de fond des montagnes.

Interiores con gusto en estilo del país y enormes mamparas que dejan la vista libre hacia el cautivador escenario de montaña.

Interni di ottimo gusto in stile tipico del paese e pareti a vetro alte fino al soffitto permettono la vista sulla splendida cornice delle montagne.

Llao Llao Resort *San Carlos de Bariloche, Argentina*

Four Seasons Resort Carmelo

Carmelo, Uruguay

The estate is like a hacienda and nestles between eucalyptus forests and the savanna, where the gauchos ride. The 20 bungalows and 24 suites, various restaurants, the lobby, a spa with health club and swimming pool all show rustic charm with lots of wood, stone and iron fretwork. But you'll also find design influences from Asia and the South Seas. All buildings have a view of the Rio de la Plata delta, one of the world's widest rivers. A sand bank that you can reach by kayak, surfboard or yacht provides a wonderful beach.

Wie eine Hazienda schmiegt sich die Anlage zwischen Eukalyptus-Wälder und die Savanne, auf der Gauchos reiten. Die 20 Bungalows und 24 Suiten, diverse Restaurants, die Lobby, ein Spa mit Health Club und Swimmingpool, zeigen rustikalen Charme mit viel Holz, Stein und geschmiedetem Eisen. Aber auch gestalterische Einflüsse aus Asien und der Südsee sind zu finden. Von allen Gebäuden geht der Blick zum Mündungsdelta des Rio de la Plata, einem der breitesten Flüsse der Welt. Eine Sandbank, die man per Kajak, Surfbrett oder Segelboot erreicht, bietet einen herrlichen Strand.

Comme une hacienda, la propriété se niche entre les forêts d'eucalyptus et la savane parcourue par les gauchos à cheval. Les 20 bungalows et les 24 suites, différents restaurants, le lobby, un spa avec health club et piscine, affichent un charme rustique avec beaucoup de bois, de la pierre et du fer forgé. Pour la conception, il s'y mêle aussi des influences asiatiques et des mers du sud. De tous les bâtiments la vue donne sur l'embouchure du delta du Rio de la Plata, l'un des fleuves les plus larges au monde. Un banc de sable auquel on accède en kayak, en planche à voile ou en voilier constitue une magnifique plage.

Una hacienda inmersa entre bosques de eucalipto y la pampa de los gauchos. El hotel cuenta con 20 bungalows y 24 suites, piscina, varios restaurantes, un hall, Spa con Health Club y piscina. Todo ello decorado con el encanto rústico que proporcionan la madera, la piedra y el hierro forjado. Aun y todo se aprecian también influencias decorativas de Asia y los Mares del Sur. Todos los edificios disfrutan de las vistas al delta del Río de la Plata, uno de los ríos más anchos del planeta. Los bancos de arena de la desembocadura forman una playa fantástica a la que se accede con kayak o barco de vela.

La struttura si poggia come una hacienda tra boschi di eucalipto e la savana, in cui cavalcano i gauchi. I 20 bungalow e le 24 suite, vari ristoranti, la lobby, una spa con health club e piscina sono arredati con gusto rustico in legno, pietra e ferro battuto. Ma sono presenti anche influssi dall'Asia e dai mari del Sud. Da tutti gli edifici si gode la vista sul delta del Rio de la Plata, uno dei più grandi fiumi del mondo. Un banco di sabbia raggiungibile con il kajak, la sailboard o la barca a vela mette a disposizione una bellissima spiaggia.

Enjoy breakfast on your private terrace, the midday sun by the pool and spend the evenings with a glass of wine by the "camp fire"; a holiday at this resort promises to be an inspiration.

Frühstück auf der eigenen Terrasse genießen, die Mittagssonne am Pool und abends ein Glas Wein am „Lagerfeuer"; der Aufenthalt in diesem Resort verspricht Inspiration.

Le petit déjeuner sur sa terrasse privée, le soleil de midi au bord de la piscine et le soir un verre de vin auprès d'un feu de camp : le séjour dans ce resort ne peut qu'inspirer.

Un resort que inspira a los sentidos: el placer de disfrutar del desayuno en la propia terraza, del sol de mediodía en la piscina, y de una copa de vino en torno a una fogata.

Fare colazione sulla terrazza privata, godere il sole del pomeriggio sui bordi della piscina e, la sera, sorseggiare un bicchiere di vino intorno al falò: il soggiorno in questo resort sarà fonte di ispirazione.

The 18-hole *golf course is nestling in the savanna's nature. It's dotted with lakes and bunkers and is certainly one of South America's most beautiful courses.*

Eingebettet in *die Natur der Savanne, unterbrochen von Seen und Bunkern, ist der 18-Loch-Kurs sicher einer der schönsten Plätze Südamerikas.*

Au cœur *de la nature de la savane, parsemé de lacs et de bunkers, le parcours 18 trous est assurément l'un des meilleurs terrains d'Amérique du sud.*

El recorrido *de 18 hoyos dibujado sobre la pampa serpenteando entre lagos y bunkers es sin duda uno de los más bellos de Sudamérica.*

Adagiato nella *natura della savana e costellato di specchi d'acqua e di bunker, il campo a 18 buche è senz'altro uno dei più bei posti del Sudamerica.*

The Gleneagles Hotel
Perthshire, Scotland

After its opening in 1924, the hotel that is built in the style of a French château quickly advanced to a social meeting place. Guests came for hunting, fishing and golf. Sean Connery (alias James Bond) put in the groundwork here for his one-figure handicap. The falconry instructs guests in this aristocratic sport, the riding school boasts a world-class standard and anyone who enjoys shooting at clay pigeons with Berettas has the best conditions for learning here. After all that, it's hardly worth mentioning that Gleneagles has an excellent spa and offers a chauffeur service to explore the nearby countryside.

Nach der Eröffnung 1924 avancierte das im Stil eines französischen Châteaus erbaute Hotel schnell zum gesellschaftlichen Treffpunkt. Man kam zum Jagen, Fischen und Golfen. Sean Connery alias James Bond hat hier die Grundlagen für sein einstelliges Handicap gelegt. Die Falknerei unterrichtet Gäste in diesem aristokratischen Sport, die Reitschule hat Weltklasse-Niveau und wer gerne mit Berettas auf Tontauben schießen möchte, kann das hier zu besten Bedingungen lernen. Da ist es kaum noch erwähnenswert, dass Gleneagles über ein ausgezeichnetes Spa und einen Chauffeur-Service zur Erkundung der näheren Umgebung verfügt.

A son ouverture en 1924 cet hôtel bâti comme un château français est vite devenu le point de rencontre de la haute société. On y venait pour chasser, pêcher et jouer au golf. Sean Connery alias James Bond y a jeté les bases de son handicap en dessous de 10. La fauconnerie initie les hôtes à ce sport aristocratique, l'école d'équitation jouit d'un niveau d'élite et ceux qui le désirent peuvent s'initier là au tir au pigeon d'argile avec des carabines Berettas dans les meilleures conditions. Inutile de mentionner que Gleneagles dispose d'un excellent spa et d'un service de chauffeur pour la découverte des environs immédiats.

Tras su apertura en 1924, este castillo de estilo francés se fue creando un estatus como centro de encuentro social. A este lugar se venía a cazar, a pescar o a jugar al golf. Sean Connery, alias James Bond, sentó aquí las bases para reducir su handicap a una cifra. Los huéspedes disfrutarán de las mejores condiciones para iniciarse en el aristocrático deporte de la cetrería, practicar la equitación a gran nivel o entretenerse con el tiro al plato. Sin olvidar que Gleneagles dispone además de un Spa excepcional y servicio de chofer para descubrir los alrededores.

Aperto nel 1924, questo hotel costruito nello stile di un castello francese divenne ben presto un punto di ritrovo sociale, con possibilità di praticare sport quali la caccia, la pesca e il golf. Sean Connery alias James Bond ha posto qui le basi per il suo bassissimo handicap. La falconeria istruisce gli ospiti in questo aristocratico sport, la scuola di equitazione è di altissimo livello e ci sono ottimi corsi anche di tiro al piattello. A questo punto, non è più necessario menzionare che Gleneagles dispone anche di un'eccellente Spa e del servizio di autista per la visita dei dintorni.

Just as the mood grabs you: enjoy a light midday lunch al fresco, dinner in the evening in a luxurious ambiance and prepared by Andrew Fairlie, one of Scotland's best head chefs.

Ganz nach Lust und Laune: Mittags legerer Lunch im Freien, abends Dinner im luxuriösen Ambiente, bekocht von Andrew Fairlie, einem der besten schottischen Küchenmeister.

Selon l'humeur et l'envie du moment: le midi, déjeuner léger á l'air libre, le soir, dîner dans une ambiance de luxe, préparé par Andrew Fairlie, l'un des meilleurs chefs cuisiniers écossais.

Según las apetencias; el almuerzo ligero al aire libre, la cena en ambiente lujoso, pero todo de la mano de uno de los grandes cocineros escoceses, Andrew Fairlie.

A capriccio: a mezzogiorno un leggero lunch nel fresco, la sera cena in ambiente lussuoso per gustare la cucina di Andrew Fairlie, uno dei migliori cuochi di Scozia.

The Gleneagles Hotel is surrounded by world-class golf courses and combines tradition with modern comfort. In summer 2005, the G8-world economic summit took place here.

Umgeben von Weltklasse-Golfplätzen, verbindet das Gleneagles Hotel Tradition mit modernem Komfort. Im Sommer 2005 fand hier der Weltwirtschaftsgipfel statt.

Entouré des terrains de golf de l'élite mondiale, l'hôtel Gleneagles associe tradition et confort moderne. En été 2005, il a hébergé le Forum Economique Mondial.

El hotel Gleneagles combina tradición y confort de hoy en torno a campos de golf de nivel internacional. En el verano de 2005 tuvo aquí lugar la Cumbre Económica Mundial.

Circondato da campi da golf di classe internazionale, l'hotel Gleneagles unisce tradizione e comfort moderno. Il G8 ha avuto luogo proprio qui nell'estate del 2005.

The Gleneagles Hotel *Perthshire, Scotland* 61

Stoke Park Club

Buckinghamshire, England

Stoke Park Club was already established in 1908 and is considered the oldest country club in Britain. The palatial building and splendid park even date back over more than nine hundred years. 21 individual guest suites are available in this stylish ambiance, which is home to a respected members-only club. The 27-hole golf course "Stoke Poges", the scene of Sean Connery's and Gert Fröbe's round of golf in "Goldfinger", regularly counted amongst the "best places". With the exclusive spa that pampers guests, Stoke Park Club has risen to the "Top Ten Golf and Spa Resorts around the World".

Bereits 1908 gegründet, gilt der Stoke Park Club als ältester Country Club des Landes. Das palastartige Gebäude und der prächtige Park blicken gar auf eine mehr als neunhundert Jahre alte Geschichte zurück. In diesem stilvollen Ambiente, das Heimat eines angesehenen Member Clubs ist, stehen 21 individuelle Gäste-Suiten zur Verfügung. Der 27-Loch-Kurs „Stoke Poges", auf dem sich Sean Connery und Gert Fröbe in „Goldfinger" ein Match lieferten, zählte regelmäßig zu den „Best Places". Zusammen mit dem exklusiven Spa, das die Gäste verwöhnt, ist der Stoke Park Club zu den „Top Ten Golf and Spa Resorts around the World" aufgestiegen.

Fondé dès 1908, le Stoke Park Club est considéré comme le plus vieux country club du pays. Le bâtiment qui ressemble à un palais et le superbe parc ont plus de neuf cents ans d'histoire. Dans cette atmosphère raffinée, pays d'origine d'un des clubs les plus prestigieux, se trouvent 21 suites individuelles. Le parcours de 27 trous « Stoke Poges » sur lequel Sean Connery et Gert Fröbe ont disputé un match dans le film « Goldfinger » a régulièrement été classé parmi les meilleurs. Avec son spa exclusif où les hôtes sont dorlotés, le Stoke Park Club s'est hissé dans les 10 premiers « Golf and Spa Resorts » au monde.

El Stoke Park Club fue edificado en 1908, lo que le ha convertido en el club de campo más antiguo del país. Se trata de una construcción palaciega en torno a un parque soberbio, que guarda en su memoria más de novecientos años de historia. Esta atmósfera cargada de estilo, hogar de un privilegiado Member Club, alberga 21 suites exclusivas. El recorrido de 27 hoyos "Stoke Poges", que fue escenario de juego entre Sean Connery y Gert Fröbe en "James Bond contra Goldfinger", contaba con frecuencia entre uno de los "Best Places". El exclusivo Spa, para mimar a los clientes, pone el toque final que ha convertido al Stoke Park Club en uno de los "Top Ten Golf and Spa Resorts around the World".

Fondato già nel 1908, lo Stoke Park Club rappresenta il country club più antico del paese. Il sontuoso edificio e lo splendido parco vantano una storia vecchia più di novecento anni. In questo ambiente di gran classe, patria di un apprezzato Member Club, sono disponibili 21 suite individuali. Il percorso a 27 buche "Stoke Poges", sul quale si sono sfidati Sean Connery e Gert Fröbe in "Goldfinger", si è sempre annoverato tra i "Best Places". Insieme all'esclusiva spa – per il benessere degli ospiti – lo Stoke Park Club si è guadagnato un posto tra i "Top Ten Golf and Spa Resorts around the World".

Furniture with comfortable cushions in front of an open fire invites guests to relax in style after a round of golf.

Dicke Polstermöbel vor dem offenen Kamin laden zum stilvollen Relaxen nach einer Runde Golf ein.

Des fauteuils bien rembourrés devant la cheminée pour une détente de bon goût après une partie de golf.

Los grandes sillones dispuestos frente a la chimenea invitan al relax tras un rato de golf.

Massicci mobili imbottiti posti intorno al caminetto invitano al relax dopo il golf in un ambiente elegante.

Heavy fabrics and pastel tones define the interior design in the suites. This fulfils guests' romantic ideals when they see the palace from the outside. By contrast, guests dine in the restaurant in a modern interior.

Schwere Stoffe und Pastelltöne bestimmen die Innenraumgestaltung der Suiten. Sie treffen damit die romantischen Vorstellungen der Gäste, wenn sie den Palast von außen sehen. Im Restaurant speist man dagegen in modernem Interieur.

De lourdes étoffes et des tons pastel caractérisent la décoration intérieure des suites. Ceci correspond au romantisme qu'imaginent les hôtes en voyant le palais de l'extérieur. Dans le restaurant cependant on mange dans un intérieur moderne.

Telas pesadas y tonos pastel decoran las suites, respondiendo perfectamente a la imagen romántica que tienen los huéspedes al ver el palacio desde el exterior. Por el contrario, el restaurante está dotado de un ambiente moderno.

Stoffe pesanti e toni pastello dominano all'interno delle suite, in armonia con l'immagine romantica degli ospiti che il palazzo mostra esternamente. Il ristorante, invece, è arredato in stile moderno.

The Grove
Hertfordshire, England

The Country House Hotel was already showered with awards only shortly after its opening in 2003. The Sequoia Spa was nominated the best spa in the United Kingdom, the golf course one of the most attractive new courses in Europe and the restaurants were given top marks. The contemporary design, which is still rare at British golf resorts, coupled with perfect service quickly made The Grove—located only 40 minutes north west of Britain's capital city—into a popular weekend stopover for London's scene.

Schon kurz nach seiner Eröffnung 2003 wurde das Country House Hotel mit Auszeichnungen überhäuft. Das Sequoia Spa wurde zum besten Spa des Vereinigten Königreichs ernannt, der Golfplatz zu einem der schönsten neuen Kurse in Europa und die Restaurants erhielten Spitzennoten. Das bei britischen Golf Resorts noch seltene, zeitgenössische Design, gepaart mit perfektem Service, machten The Grove – nur 40 Minuten nordwestlich der britischen Hauptstadt gelegen – schnell zur Wochenend-Lieblingsadresse der Londoner Szene.

Peu après son ouverture en 2003 le Country House Hotel a collectionné les distinctions. Le Spa Sequoia a été déclaré meilleur spa du Royaume Uni, le terrain de golf classé parmi les meilleurs nouveaux golfs d'Europe et les restaurants ont obtenu les meilleures notes. Le design contemporain qui est encore rare dans les golf-resorts britanniques, associé à un service parfait a rapidement fait de The Grove – à seulement 40 minutes au nord-ouest de la capitale britannique – l'adresse de fin de semaine préférée de la scène londonienne.

Apenas inaugurado en 2003, al Country House Hotel le llovieron los galardones: su Spa Secuoya obtuvo el título al mejor Spa del Reino Unido. Al campo de golf se le cuenta entre uno de los más bellos de Europa y sus restaurantes han obtenido las más altas calificaciones. El diseño contemporáneo, aún una excepción en los resorts de golf británicos, ligado a un servicio perfecto, han convertido al The Grove en la opción preferida para el fin de semana de la alta sociedad londinense, especialmente teniendo en cuenta que está a sólo 40 minutos al noroeste de la capital.

Già subito dopo l'apertura nel 2003, l'hotel Country House è stato insignito di molti premi. La Sequoia Spa è stata eletta migliore Spa del Regno Unito, il campo da golf uno dei più bei percorsi d'Europa e i ristoranti hanno ottenuto voti altissimi. Il design moderno, ancora raro nei resort golfistici inglesi, unito al servizio perfetto, hanno presto fatto di The Grove – a soli 40 minuti a nord-ovest della capitale inglese – una delle mete preferite dal jet-set londinese per il fine settimana.

The British firm Fox Linton Associates is responsible for the stylish, modern design behind the historical walls.

Für das schicke, moderne Design hinter den geschichtsträchtigen Mauern steht die britische Firma Fox Linton Associates.

Le design moderne et chic derrière ces murs chargés d'histoire est signé de la société britannique Fox Linton Associates.

Fox Linton Associates es la responsable del diseño moderno y elegante que esconde el histórico edificio.

Il design moderno ed elegante che si cela all'interno delle mura cariche di storia è opera della società inglese Fox Linton Associates.

The 227 *rooms offer a mix of tradition, glamour and country style, but especially comfort, quality and relaxation.*

Die 227 *Zimmer bieten eine Mischung aus Tradition, Glamour und Country-Style, vor allem jedoch Komfort, Qualität und Entspannung.*

Les 227 *chambres conjuguent tradition, style glamour et charme rural mais surtout confort, qualité et détente.*

Las 227 *habitaciones son un conjunto de glamour y estilo de campo bajo el lema del confort, la calidad y el relax.*

Le 227 *camere offrono una combinazione di tradizione, fascino e stile country, ma soprattutto comfort, qualità e distensione.*

From the outside it's old and refined, from the inside young and hip—the entire resort is set in one of Europe's most beautiful golf courses.

Von außen alt und erhaben, innen jung und hip, das Ganze umrahmt von einem der schönsten Golfplätze Europas.

A l'extérieur vieux et noble, à l'intérieur jeune et enjoué, le tout entouré d'un des plus beaux parcours de golf d'Europe.

Un exterior antiguo y sublime; un interior joven y actual; y como escenario uno de los campos de golf más bellos de Europa.

Esternamente antico e imponente, all'interno giovane ed esclusivo: il tutto circondato da uno dei più bei campi da golf europei.

Marriott Druids Glen Hotel & Country Club

County Wicklow, Ireland

The old clubhouse of Druid's Glen is located only 20 miles south of Dublin and nestles in the mystical landscape between the Irish Sea and the Wicklow mountains. It lies harmonious in the close neighbourhood of the new Marriott Hotel, which offers its guests luxury spa and conference center. This mix of tradition and modernity has its own unique charm. That explains the hotel's nomination as "European Golf Resort of the Year 2005", which is obviously also because of the two tournament golf courses, even if the guests can equally enjoy fly fishing and riding here.

Eingebettet in die mystische Landschaft zwischen Irischer See und den Wicklow Mountains, dabei nur 32 Kilometer südlich von Dublin, liegt das alte Clubhaus von Druids Glen in einträchtiger Nachbarschaft mit dem neuen Marriott Hotel, dem ein luxuriöses Spa und ein Konferenzcenter angeschlossen sind. Dieser Mix von Tradition und Moderne hat seinen ganz eigenen Reiz. Das zeigt sich auch daran, dass das Hotel zum „European Golf Resort of the Year 2005" gewählt wurde, was natürlich auch an den beiden Turnier-Golfplätzen liegt, obwohl man hier genauso gut Fliegenfischen und Reiten kann.

Dans ce paysage mystique entre la mer d'Irlande et les montagnes du Wicklow, mais à seulement 32 kilomètres au sud de Dublin, le vieux club-house du Druids Glen affiche un voisinage harmonieux avec le nouvel hôtel Marriott, flanqué d'une aile abritant un luxueux spa et un centre de conférence. Le mariage de la tradition et du moderne revêt un charme tout particulier. Ce que démontre l'élection de « Golf-Resort Européen de l'Année 2005 » justifiée aussi, bien sûr, par les deux parcours de championnat, même si dans cet endroit on peut également pêcher à la mouche et faire de l'équitation.

A sólo 32 kilómetros al sur de Dublín, un paisaje místico entre el Mar de Irlanda y la cordillera Wicklow envuelve al antiguo Clubhouse de Druids Glen ubicado armónicamente junto al nuevo hotel Marriott y su lujoso Spa y centro de conferencias. El resultado es una atrayente y exclusiva combinación de tradición y modernidad. No sin motivo ha sido galardonado con el título "European Golf Resort of the Year 2005", a lo que contribuyen claramente sus dos campos de golf de torneo. Aunque la pesca con mosca y la equitación son también parte del atractivo del lugar.

Adagiato nel paesaggio mistico tra il Mare d'Irlanda e le Wicklow Mountains, a soli 32 chilometri a sud di Dublino, si trova l'antico cubhouse di Druids Glen, piacevolmente vicino al nuovo hotel Marriott, a cui sono annessi una lussuosa spa ed un centro congressi. Questa combinazione di tradizione e modernità ha un fascino tutto particolare. Lo dimostra anche il fatto che questo hotel è stato eletto "European Golf Resort of the Year 2005": merito, naturalmente, anche dei due campi da golf da torneo, sebbene qui, allo stesso modo, sia pure possibile praticare la pesca a mosca o cavalcare.

Irish country style: a cozy evening in front of a roaring fire after a round on the golf course.

Irischer Country-Style: Nach einer Runde auf dem Golfplatz folgt der gemütliche Abend vor dem knisternden Kamin.

Le charme rural irlandais : après une partie de golf, une soirée tranquille au coin d'un feu de cheminée crépitant.

El estilo de la campiña irlandesa: un rato de golf seguido de una velada relajante al calor y chisporroteo de la chimenea.

Stile country irlandese: dopo una partita a golf, segue la piacevole serata davanti al caminetto scoppiettante.

A successful combination: traditional clubhouse with modern hotel, with the highlight being two Masters golf courses.

Eine gelungene Verbindung: traditionelles Clubhaus mit modernem Hotel, gekrönt von zwei Meisterschaftsgolfplätzen.

Une association réussie : le club-house traditionnel et l'hôtel moderne, couronnés par deux parcours de championnat.

Un enlace perfecto entre club de campo tradicional y hotel moderno al abrigo de dos campos de golf de torneo.

Una combinazione riuscita: clubhouse tradizionale ed hotel moderno, il tutto coronato da due campi da golf da campionato.

Adare Manor Hotel & Golf Resort
Adare, Ireland

The estate was built as a manor house around 1832 and it is fairly eccentric: an entrance tower, decorated with gargoyles, pinnacles and 52 chimneys, dominates it. Out of the 365 windows, you can look at the splendid golf course, wild river and luscious green parkland from a different perspective every single day of the year. The interior is also unusual, with the Minstrel's Gallery, an intimation of Versailles's Hall of Mirrors, being the most impressive and measuring over 130 feet long and 26 feet high.

Das um 1832 als Rittergut erbaute Anwesen ist ziemlich exzentrisch: dominiert von einem Eingangsturm, bestückt mit Wasserspeiern, Zinnen und 52 Kaminen. Aus 365 Fenstern kann man an jedem Tag im Jahr den herrlichen Golfplatz, den wilden Fluss und den saftig grünen Park aus einer anderen Perspektive betrachten. Auch das Interieur ist ungewöhnlich, wobei die Minstrel's Gallery, eine Nachahmung des Versailler Spiegelsaales, mit über 40 Metern Länge und acht Metern Höhe wohl am eindrucksvollsten ist.

Cette gentilhommière bâtie vers 1832 est assez excentrique : dominée par une tour crénelée, ornée de gargouilles, de créneaux et de 52 cheminées. De 365 fenêtres on peut admirer le magnifique golf, la rivière sauvage et le parc verdoyant d'un point de vue chaque jour différent. L'intérieur du manoir est également inhabituel : ainsi, la salle Minstrel inspirée par la galerie des glaces de Versailles est la plus impressionnante avec plus de 40 mètre de long et huit mètre de hauteur.

Una propiedad señorial construida en 1832 y cargada de excentricidad. El edificio está dominado por una torreta de entrada y revestido con gárgolas, almenas y 52 chimeneas. Sus 365 ventanas bastan para admirar desde diferentes perspectivas el fantástico campo de golf, el río bravo y el verdor del parque durante todo el año. También su interior está fuera de lo común. Y sin duda la Minstrel's Gallery, una imitación de la sala de los espejos de Versalles de más 40 metros de largo y ocho de alto, es la estancia más impresionante.

La struttura, costruita intorno al 1832 come residenza feudale, è piuttosto inusuale: dominata da una torre d'entrata e sormontata da doccioni, merli e 52 camini. Dalle 365 finestre si possono ammirare il magnifico campo da golf, il tumultuoso fiume ed il parco lussureggiante da una prospettiva diversa ogni giorno dell'anno. Anche gli interni sono fuori dal comune: tra essi spicca la Minstrel's Gallery, un'imitazione della sala degli specchi di Versailles, alta otto metri e lunga più di 40.

Two restaurants cater with their culinary selection for the resort's guests. The guest rooms and suites are spread about the Manor House, Clubhouse, Townhouse and several villas.

Zwei Restaurants versorgen die Gäste des Resorts mit ihrem kulinarischen Angebot. Die Gästezimmer und Suiten verteilen sich auf das Manor House, Clubhouse, Townhouse und mehrere Villen.

Deux restaurants régalent les hôtes du resort avec leur talent culinaire. Les chambres d'hôtes et les suites sont réparties dans le manoir, le club-house, la town-house et plusieurs villas.

La amplia oferta gastronómica está presente en los dos restaurantes del resort. Los tres edificios, Manor House, Clubhouse y Townhouse albergan habitaciones, si bien también hay villas separadas disponibles.

Due ristoranti offrono agli ospiti le loro specialità gastronomiche. Le camere e le suite si trovano nella Manor House, nel Clubhouse, nella Townhouse ed in diverse ville.

The suites *are decorated in the style of a previous era: slightly plush materials, but refined and spacious at the same time.*

Die Suiten *zeigen sich im Stil einer vergangenen Epoche: leicht plüschig, gleichzeitig aber edel und großzügig.*

Les suites *affichent le style d'une époque révolue : légèrement désuet, en même temps noble et généreux.*

Las suites *retienen el estilo de épocas pasadas, ligeramente aburguesado pero elegante y espléndido.*

Le suite *sono arredate nello stile di un' epoca passata: leggermente demodè, ma al tempo stesso eleganti e spaziose.*

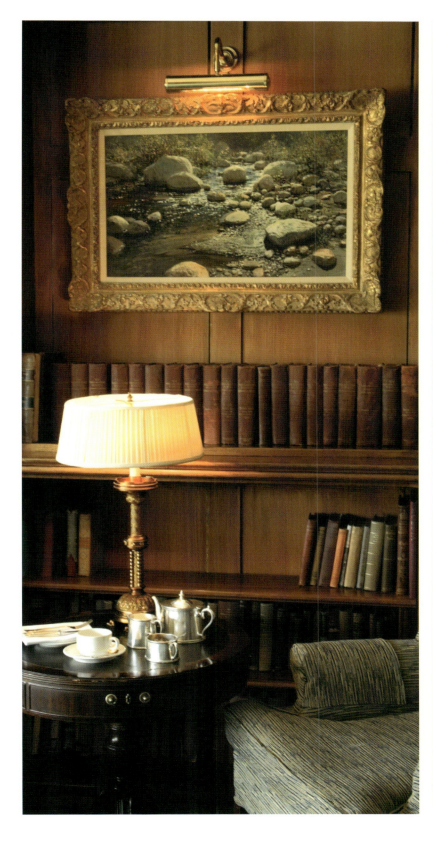

Dromoland Castle
County Clare, Ireland

This is how you imagine a Celtic nobleman's castle—exactly like this and without changing a single thing. The castle is imposing, with thick towers, pinnacles and bay windows and it's located in breathtaking countryside. Built in the 16th century, Dromoland Castle was once home to the O'Brien family, one of the noblest Irish clans. If you enter the Castle hotel today—naturally stepping on the red carpet—the atmosphere of aristocratic refinement unmistakably confronts you. You can feel it in the historic ambiance of the rooms and the friendly, discreet service.

Genau so und nicht anders stellt man sich das Schloss eines keltischen Edelmanns vor. Imposant, mit dicken Türmen, Zinnen und Erkern, liegt es in einer atemberaubenden Landschaft. Erbaut im 16. Jahrhundert, war Dromoland Castle einst Heim der O'Brien Familie, einem der nobelsten irischen Clans. Betritt man das Schlosshotel heute – selbstverständlich über einen roten Teppich – schlägt einem unverkennbar die Atmosphäre adliger Kultiviertheit entgegen. Sie ist im historischen Ambiente der Räume sowie im freundlichen, unaufdringlichen Service zu spüren.

C'est ainsi et pas autrement que l'on imagine le château d'un gentilhomme celte. Imposant, avec d'épaisses tours et créneaux, des pièces en saillie, il se dresse dans un paysage à couper le souffle. Bâti au 16ème siècle, le Dromoland Castle était jadis la demeure de la famille O'Brien, l'un des clans irlandais les plus nobles. En pénétrant aujourd'hui dans ce château transformé en hôtel – évidemment sur un tapis rouge – on est enveloppé d'une atmosphère de culture aristocratique. Elle se ressent dans l'ambiance des pièces chargées d'histoire et dans le service chaleureux et discret.

No existe mejor imagen que describa el castillo de un noble celta. Imponente, con sus almenas y torres masivas, bajo el escenario de un paisaje embriagador. Dromoland Castle fue construido en el siglo XVI como hogar de la familia O'Brien, uno de los clanes más nobles de Irlanda. Hoy al entrar al castillo, pisando la ineludible alfombra roja, invade una atmósfera de nobleza cultivada, que se respira en el ambiente histórico de las habitaciones y en un servicio correcto y agradable.

Esattamente così ci si immagina il castello di un nobile celtico: imponente, con torri massicce, merli e balconcini, immerso in un paesaggio di grande bellezza. Costruito nel 16° secolo, Dromoland Castle era una volta la dimora della famiglia O'Brien, uno dei più nobili clan irlandesi. Chi entra oggi in questo hotel – naturalmente su un tappeto rosso – viene colto da un'inconfondibile atmosfera di nobile raffinatezza, riconoscibile nelle sale cariche di storia e nella cortesia e discrezione del servizio.

After its renovation costing five million Euros, the golf course, which opened in 1962, is popularly known as "Ireland's Augusta".

Der 1962 eröffnete Golfplatz wird nach seiner fünf Millionen Euro teuren Renovierung gerne als „Augusta von Irland" bezeichnet.

Ouvert en 1962, le golf est souvent qualifié « d' Augusta d'Irlande» depuis sa rénovation à hauteur de cinq millions d'euros.

El campo de golf fue inaugurado en 1962. Tras una costosa renovación de cinco millones de euros gusta llamarle "Augusta de Irlanda".

Dopo la ristrutturazione – del valore di cinque milioni di euro – il campo da golf, aperto nel 1962, è stato denominato „Augusta d'Irlanda".

The décor in the 75 rooms and 21 suites is traditional and with a floral design, while the spa has a modern character.

Die Einrichtung der 75 Zimmer und 21 Suiten ist traditionell und mit Blumenmustern dekoriert, während das Spa einen modernen Charakter hat.

La décoration des 75 chambres et 21 suites reste traditionnelle avec des motifs à fleurs, tandis que le spa affiche un caractère moderne.

La decoración de sus 75 habitaciones y 21 suites se centra en el tradicional y estampado de flores mientras que el Spa guarda un carácter moderno.

L'arredamento delle 75 camere e delle 21 suite è tradizionale, con motivi floreali, mentre la spa è di gusto moderno.

The K Club Golf Resort
County Kildare, Ireland

Just driving through the parkland and estate already promises a grand entry. When you step inside the hotel building, a hint of an aristocratic past floats your way and you even feel a little like the owner of a country estate yourself. In fact, in the year 550, this Irish country estate was home to the ancestors of King John of England and his brother Richard the Lionheart. Nowadays, international club members and hotel guests occupy the rooms that are furnished with antiques and precious oil paintings in the spirit of "noblesse oblige". The 555 acres park borders directly on the Liffey river and connects the resort with the two golf courses, designed by Arnold Palmer—and the venue for the 2006 Ryder Cup.

Schon die Auffahrt durch die Parkanlage verspricht einen großen Auftritt. Betritt man das Hotelgebäude, weht dem Besucher der Hauch adliger Vergangenheit entgegen und man fühlt sich selbst ein wenig als Großgrundbesitzer. Tatsächlich war der irische Landsitz im Jahr 550 das Heim der Vorfahren König John's von England und seinem Bruder Richard Löwenherz. Heute bewohnen internationale Clubmitglieder und Hotelgäste die Räume, die gemäß des Anspruchs „Noblesse oblige" mit antikem Mobiliar und kostbaren Ölgemälden ausgestattet sind. Der 225 Hektar große Park grenzt direkt an den Fluss Liffey und verbindet das Resort mit den zwei, von Arnold Palmer entworfenen, Golfplätzen – Austragungsort des Ryder Cup 2006.

L'accès à la demeure à travers le parc promet déjà une grande entrée en scène. Quand il pénètre dans le bâtiment, l'hôte perçoit le souffle d'une noblesse passée et se sent devenir un peu propriétaire terrien. En effet la propriété irlandaise était en 550 la demeure des ancêtres du Roi Jean d'Angleterre et de son frère Richard Cœur de Lion. Aujourd'hui des membres de clubs internationaux et des visiteurs habitent ces pièces qui, conformément à la devise « Noblesse oblige », contiennent des meubles anciens et de précieuses peintures à l'huile. Le parc de 225 hectares longe la rivière Liffey et relie le resort aux deux parcours de golf dessinés par Arnold Palmer où se déroulera la Ryder Cup en 2006.

Ya la entrada a través del parque promete grandeza. Y efectivamente, nada más acceder al edificio un aire de pasado noble se hace con el entorno y lleva incluso a imaginarse ser dueño del lugar. De hecho, en el año 550 el castillo perteneció a los antepasados del rey Juan Sin Tierra de Inglaterra y su hermano Ricardo I Corazón de León. Hoy son miembros del club y huéspedes de todo el mundo los que ocupan las suntuosas habitaciones equipadas con antigüedades y exquisitos lienzos, según los cánones de la "Noblesse oblige". El vasto parque de 225 hectáreas limita con el río Liffey y une los dos campos de golf, diseño de Arnold Palmer, que albergarán la Ryder Cup de 2006.

L'entrata attraverso il parco non deluderà le aspettative. Chi entra nell'hotel, viene colto da un'atmosfera di nobile passato, e l'ospite si sente un po' protagonista di questo ambiente aristocratico. Effettivamente, nel 550 la tenuta irlandese è stata la dimora degli antenati di re Giovanni d'Inghilterra e di suo fratello Riccardo Cuor di Leone. Oggi soci internazionali del club e ospiti dell'hotel occupano le sale che, rispondendo alle esigenze del motto "Noblesse oblige", sono arredate con mobili antichi e preziosi dipinti a olio. Il parco, che si estende su 225 ettari, è delimitato dal fiume Liffey e collega il resort con due campi da golf – teatro della Ryder Cup 2006 – progettati da Arnold Palmer.

There's one of the most beautiful views through the window. But the hotel is also like an art gallery with its extensive collection of paintings and antiques and it's well worth a visit.

Eines der schönsten Bilder bietet sich beim Blick aus dem Fenster. Mit seiner umfangreichen Gemälde- und Antiquitätensammlung ist das Hotel aber auch eine sehenswerte Kunstgalerie.

L'un des plus beaux tableaux, c'est la vue de la fenêtre. Avec son importante collection de peintures et d'antiquités, l'hôtel en soi est une remarquable galerie d'art.

Desde la ventana se abarca una hermosa vista, si bien no lo es menos la amplia colección de pinturas y antigüedades que hacen del castillo una verdadera galería de arte.

Guardando dalla finestra si gode uno dei più bei panorami mai visti. Con la sua vasta collezione di quadri e di antichità, l'hotel rappresenta tuttavia anche un'interessante galleria d'arte.

A clubby atmosphere is notable in the library, various salons or the private dining rooms.
Clubatmosphäre herrscht in der Bibliothek, diversen Salons oder den privaten Speiseräumen.
Il règne une atmosphère de club dans la bibliothèque, les divers salons et les salles à manger privées.
En la biblioteca, los salones y comedores privados domina el ambiente de club selecto.
Un'atmosfera da Club regna nella biblioteca, nei diversi saloni e nelle sale da pranzo private.

The K Club Golf Resort *County Kildare, Ireland*

Although the Irish country estate radiates respectability, it's equipped with every modern comfort. The modern design of the K Spa not only has spacious treatment rooms but also an indoor swimming pool measuring over 54 feet long.

Der irische Landsitz strahlt zwar Altehrwürdigkeit aus, doch ist er mit modernstem Komfort ausgestattet. Neben großzügigen Behandlungsräumen verfügt das modern gestaltete K Spa auch über ein 16,5 Meter langes Hallenschwimmbecken.

La demeure irlandaise a certes un aspect imposant, mais elle est dotée de tout le confort moderne. Outre de spacieuses salles de soins, le K Spa de conception moderne dispose d'une piscine couverte de 16,5 m de long.

Esta propiedad irlandesa irradia toda la dignidad de tiempos pasados sin despreciar el confort de hoy. El Spa K cuenta con amplias salas de tratamiento y una piscina cubierta de 16,5 metros de longitud.

La tenuta irlandese irradia austerità, però è dotata di oghi ccomfort moderno. Oltre agli spaziosi saloni per il trattamento, la moderna K Spa dispone anche di una piscina coperta lunga più di 16,5 metri.

Mount Juliet Conrad
County Kilkenny, Ireland

Old and new. Traditional and modern. In the 18th century Georgian Old Manor House you feel as though you are a guest in the private rooms of the Earl of Carrick and his wife, Juliet. It can't have looked much different in their day. The neighboring Courtyard Rooms are decorated in modern style and the Rose Garden Lodges look quite romantic. You have a view from all the buildings of the pleasant countryside, the River Nore and the Masters golf course, designed by Jack Nicklaus and already the venue for the Irish Open on several occasions.

Alt und neu. Traditionell und modern. Im georgianischen Old Manor House aus dem 18. Jahrhundert fühlt man sich, als wäre man in den privaten Räumen des Earls of Carrick und seiner Gemahlin Juliet zu Gast. Viel anders kann es damals nicht ausgesehen haben. Die benachbarten Courtyard Rooms sind modern eingerichtet, ganz romantisch zeigen sich die Rose Garden Lodges. Von allen Gebäuden hat man Aussicht auf die liebliche Landschaft, den River Nore und den von Jack Nicklaus konzipierten Meisterschaftsplatz, der schon mehrere Male Austragungsort für die Irish Open war.

Ancien et nouveau. Traditionnel et moderne. Dans cette demeure géorgienne de style Old Manor House du 18ème siècle on est comme invité dans les appartements privés du Comte de Carrick et de son épouse Juliet. Le cadre d'alors ne devait pas être bien différent. Les chambres de la CourtYard attenante sont aménagées de façon moderne alors que les Rose Garden Lodges sont très romantiques. Tous les bâtiments offrent une vue sur un paysage harmonieux, la rivière Nore et le golf de championnat dessiné par Jack Nicklaus et qui fut l'hôte de l'Irish Open à de nombreuses reprises.

Antiguo y nuevo. Tradicional y moderno. Una Old Manor House de estilo georgiano del siglo XVIII, que hace sentirse como si se fuera un invitado en las estancias privadas de Earls of Carrick y su esposa Juliet. Probablemente entonces su aspecto no era muy diferente. Las Courtyard Rooms vecinas están dotadas de un equipamiento moderno. El toque romántico lo proporcionan las habitaciones en los Rose Garden Lodges. Todos los edificios tienen vistas al magnífico paisaje, al río Nore y al campo de torneo concebido por Jack Nicklaus, que en más de una ocasión ha sido sede del Irish Open.

Antico e nuovo. Tradizionale e moderno. Nella georgiana Old Manor House, risalente al 18° secolo, ci si sente come ospiti nelle sale private del duca di Carrick e della sua consorte Juliet. A quei tempi non poteva essere molto diverso. Le attigue Courtyard Room sono arredate in stile moderno, mentre le Rose Garden Lodge sono squisitamente romantiche. Da tutti gli edifici si gode la vista del ridente paesaggio, del fiume Nore e del campo da golf da campionato disegnato da Jack Nicklaus, che già più volte ha accolto gli Irish Open.

30 rooms, two suites: occasionally, the best players in the world are guests here.

30 Zimmer, zwei Suiten: Ab und zu sind hier die besten Spieler der Welt zu Gast.

30 chambres, deux suites: parfois les meilleurs joueurs du monde en sont les hôtes.

30 habitaciones y dos suites cuyos huéspedes son a veces los mejores jugadores del mundo.

30 camere, due suite: di quando in quando i migliori giocatori del mondo sono ospiti di questo hotel.

Mount Juliet House is located on a slight hill with a view of the River Nore, where the salmon swim.
Mount Juliet House liegt auf einer kleinen Anhöhe mit Blick auf den River Nore, in dem Lachse schwimmen.
L'hôtel Mount Juliet est situé sur une petite hauteur avec vue sur la rivière Nore où nagent des saumons.
Mount Juliet House está ubicada sobre una elevación con vistas al río Nore, selecto refugio de salmones.
Mount Juliet House sorge su una piccola altura con vista sul fiume Nore, dalle acque ricche di salmoni.

First tea in the Morning Room, then a relaxed browse through a newspaper in one of the salons.
Erst Tee im Morning Room, dann gemütlich eine Zeitung lesen in einem der Salons.
Un thé tout d'abord dans le Morning Room puis lecture tranquille du journal dans l'un des salons.
La hora del té en el Morning Room, y leer tranquilamente el periódico en uno de los salones.
Prima un thè nella Morning Room, poi la piacevole lettura del giornale in uno dei saloni.

Der Öschberghof
Donaueschingen, Germany

The air is pure and fresh. The rising sun bathes the soft, undulating landscape of the Black Forest district of Schwarzwald-Baar and the lush green on the 27-hole golf course in a golden light. The flat, multi-sectioned building complex blends into the landscape unobtrusively. This harmony is continued in the interior. In the foyer, guests are greeted by discreet elegance. The rooms have a calm atmosphere due to the warm earth tones like ochre and brown and the equally clear lines of the design.

Die Luft ist rein und frisch. Die aufgehende Sonne taucht die sanfte Hügellandschaft des Schwarzwald-Baar-Kreises und das satte Grün des 27-Loch-Golfplatzes in ein goldenes Licht. Der flache, mehrteilige Gebäudekomplex passt sich unaufdringlich der Landschaft an. Diese Harmonie findet ihre Fortsetzung im Interieur. Diskrete Eleganz empfängt den Gast im Entrée. Warme Erdfarben wie Ocker und Braun verleihen den Räumen eine ruhige Atmosphäre, ebenso die klare Linienführung des Designs.

L'air est pur et frais. Le soleil levant éclaire d'une lumière dorée les douces collines de la Forêt Noire et de la Baar et l'étendue verdoyante du golf de 27 trous. Le complexe plat composé de plusieurs bâtiments s'intègre discrètement dans le paysage. Cette harmonie se retrouve également à l'intérieur. Une élégance sobre reçoit l'hôte dans l'entrée. Des couleurs chaudes comme l'ocre et le marron ainsi que la pureté de ligne du design confèrent aux pièces une atmosphère de calme.

En la región de Schwarzwald-Baar el aire es puro y fresco; el sol se esconde suavemente entre un paisaje de colinas, cubriendo el verde del campo de 27 hoyos con una luz dorada. El complejo de varios edificios se adapta como un guante al paisaje. La armonía se traslada al interior ya desde la discreta elegancia del vestíbulo. Los tonos ocres y marrones cálidos y las líneas claras del diseño aportan un ambiente de tranquilidad.

L'aria è pulita e fresca. Il sole che sorge spande luce dorata sul dolce paesaggio collinoso della regione di Schwarzwald-Baar e sul verde intenso del campo da golf a 27 buche. Il basso complesso di edifici, composto da più costruzioni, si adatta con discrezione al paesaggio. Questa armonia prosegue anche negli interni: una sobria eleganza accoglie l'ospite all'ingresso. I caldi colori della terra, come l'ocra e il marrone, e le linee schiette del design conferiscono alle sale un'atmosfera di relax.

The spacious lounge with fresh, modern, interior architecture matches the generosity and style of the entire resort.

Die Weiträumigkeit der Lounge, in frischer, moderner Innenarchitektur, entspricht der Großzügigkeit und dem Stil des gesamten Resorts.

L'entrée est très vaste, à l'architecture aérée et moderne ; ceci reflète bien la générosité et le style de cet ensemble.

La amplitud del salón y su arquitectura interior moderna y ligera son ejemplo claro de la esplendidez y estilo del resort.

La vastità della lounge, con la sua architettura d'interni fresca e moderna, è in sintonia con la spaziosità e lo stile dell'intero resort.

Not only *the golf course is especially interesting for golfers, but also the fitness center with its minimalist design and measuring 400 m², as well as the adjoining sports institute with medical programs.*

Nicht nur *der Golfplatz, auch das minimalistisch gestaltete, 400 m² große Wellnesszentrum sowie das angeschlossene Sport-Institut mit medizinischen Programmen, ist für Golfspieler besonders beachtenswert.*

Le terrain *de golf, mais aussi le centre de remise en forme à la conception minimaliste, occupant 400 m² ainsi que l'institut de sport attenant proposant des programmes de soins médicaux sont particulièrement attrayants pour les golfeurs.*

Además de *un centro Wellness de 400 m² de concepción minimalista, el instituto deportivo adjunto y sus programas médicos son un foco más de atracción para los amantes del golf.*

Non soltanto *il campo da golf, ma anche il centro wellness in stile minimalistico, che occupa una superficie di 400 m², e l'annesso istituto sportivo con programmi medici, sono di grande interesse per i giocatori di golf.*

Der Öschberghof *Donaueschingen, Germany*

Schlosshotel Friedrichsruhe

Friedrichsruhe, Germany

This place has retained its historic charm. Once, hunting guests of the royal family of Hohenlohe used to spend the night here; nowadays Castle Friedrichsruhe, built in 1712, is an elegant hotel. Above all, it's famous for Lothar Eiermann's cuisine. He's one of Germany's best chefs. The ensemble of hunting lodge, gate house, summer house and a building dating from the 1960s is located in the middle of a pastoral idyll in the Hohenlohe region, surrounded by an extensive park in the immediate vicinity of the Heilbronn-Hohenlohe Golf Club.

Ein Haus, das sich seinen historischen Charme erhalten hat. Einst nächtigten hier die Jagdgäste der fürstlichen Familie zu Hohenlohe, heute ist das 1712 erbaute Schloss Friedrichsruhe ein elegantes Hotel, bekannt vor allem durch Lothar Eiermanns Küche, in Deutschland einer der besten Köche. Das Ensemble aus Jagdschloss, Torhaus, Gartenhaus und einem Gebäude aus den sechziger Jahren, liegt inmitten der ländlichen Idylle des Hohenloher Landes, umgeben von einem weitläufigen Park und in unmittelbarer Nachbarschaft zum Golf-Club Heilbronn-Hohenlohe.

Une résidence qui a conservé son charme d'antan. Jadis y séjournaient les hôtes de chasse du Prince zu Hohenlohe ; aujourd'hui le château Friedrichsruhe construit en 1712 est un élégant hôtel, surtout connu pour la cuisine de Lothar Eiermann, l'un des meilleurs cuisiniers allemands. La propriété constituée d'un pavillon de chasse, d'une maison fortifiée, d'une maison de jardin et d'un bâtiment datant des années 60 se niche dans la campagne idyllique de la région de Hohenlohe, entourée d'un immense parc et à proximité immédiate du Golf-Club Heilbronn-Hohenlohe.

Esta casa ha sabido mantener su encanto histórico. En su día pernoctaban aquí los invitados a cazar de la familia Hohenlohe. Actualmente el castillo Friedrichsruhe, construido en 1712, es un elegante hotel que debe su prestigio en gran medida al arte gastronómico de Lothar Eiermann, uno de los grandes cocineros de Alemania. El conjunto de edificios está compuesto por el pabellón de caza, el porche, el pabellón de jardín y un edificio de los años sesenta, todo ello ubicado en el marco idílico del paisaje de Hohenlohe y rodeado por un gran parque vecino al club de golf Heilbronn-Hohenlohe.

Una struttura che ha mantenuto il proprio fascino storico. Una volta pernottavano qui gli ospiti di caccia della famiglia dei principi zu Hohenlohe; oggi Schloss Friedrichsruhe, costruito nel 1712, è un elegante hotel, noto soprattutto per la cucina di Lothar Eiermann, uno dei migliori cuochi della Germania. L'insieme di edifici composto da castello di caccia, portineria, dépendance ed un edificio risalente agli anni sessanta, è immerso nel bucolico idillio della regione di Hohenlohe, circondato da un vasto parco nelle immediate vicinanze del club golfistico Heilbronn-Hohenlohe.

The Castle Hotel Friedrichsruhe has been part of the "Relais & Châteaux" group since 1963 and this makes it the group's oldest German member.

Seit 1963 gehört das Schlosshotel Friedrichsruhe der Vereinigung „Relais & Châteaux" an und ist damit deren ältestes deutsches Mitglied.

Depuis 1963 le Schlosshotel Friedrichsruhe appartient à l'association «Relais & Châteaux » dont il est le membre allemand le plus ancien.

Desde 1963 el castillo hotel Friedrichsruhe es miembro de la asociación "Relais & Châteaux", y con ello el más antiguo de Alemania.

Dal 1963 il Schlosshotel Friedrichsruhe appartiene all'associazione "Relais & Châteaux" e ne è quindi il socio tedesco più anziano.

Every room carries the signature of Princess Katharina zu Hohenlohe-Öhringen and is furnished with precious, antique family furniture.

Jeder Raum trägt die Handschrift der Fürstin Katharina zu Hohenlohe-Öhringen und ist mit kostbaren antiken Möbeln der Familie ausgestattet.

Chaque pièce porte la signature de la princesse Katharina zu Hohenlohe-Öhringen et est aménagée avec des meubles antiques précieux de la famille.

Cada una de las estancias lleva el sello personal de la princesa Catarina de Hohenlohe-Öhringen y está dotada con exquisitos muebles antiguos de la familia.

Ogni sala è firmata della principessa Katharina zu Hohenlohe-Öhringen ed è arredata con preziosi mobili antichi di proprietà della famiglia.

Palazzo Arzaga Hotel Spa & Golf Resort
Lake Garda, Italy

What about living and playing golf like an Italian baron? The ambiance of the family-owned Palazzo Arzaga near Lake Garda is almost destined for this. The first-class hotel, spa and golf resort combines tradition and modernity in a charming way. The rooms in the 15th century palace—partly with frescoes dating from this period—are decorated with antique furniture and also offer satellite TV and internet connection. Both golf courses are designed by Jack Nicklaus II and Gary Player—each golfer was a master of this sport. Altogether, they provide the best conditions for a stylish "dolce far niente".

Wohnen und Golfen wie ein italienischer Baron? Das Ambiente des familieneigenen Palazzo Arzaga nahe dem Gardasee ist dazu prädestiniert. Das erstklassige Hotel, Spa und Golf Resort, verbindet in charmanter Weise Tradition und Moderne. Die Räume des Palasts aus dem 15. Jahrhundert – zum Teil noch mit Fresken aus dieser Zeit – sind mit antiken Möbeln eingerichtet und bieten gleichzeitig Satelliten-TV und ISDN-Anschluss. Die beiden Golfplätze sind von Jack Nicklaus II und Gary Player gestaltet, jeder ein Meister in diesem Fach. Alles zusammen ergibt die besten Voraussetzungen für ein stilvolles „dolce far niente".

Résider et jouer au golf comme un baron italien ? Le cadre du Palazzo Arzaga, propriété familiale, près du Lac de Garde, semble y être prédestiné. Cet hôtel de luxe avec spa et golf resort allie avec charme tradition et modernisme. Les pièces de ce palais du 15ème siècle – avec certaines fresques d'origine – sont amanagées de meubles antiques mais aussi dotées des télévision par satellite et liaison ISDN. Les deux parcours de golf ont été tracés par Jack Nicklaus II et Gary Player, tous deux maîtres en la matière. Le tout créant les conditions d'un doux farniente de bon goût.

¿Y por qué no alojarse y jugar al golf como un barón italiano? Sin duda el ambiente del Palazzo familiar Arzaga, cercano al lago de Garda está predestinado a ello. En el exclusivo resort con hotel, Spa y centro de golf concuerdan tradición y modernidad. Las habitaciones de este palacio del siglo XV, algunas de ellas aún con frescos de la época y todas decoradas con antigüedades, cuentan a la vez con televisión vía satélite y conexión RDSI. Ambos campos de golf son diseño de dos maestros en la materia: Jack Nicklaus II y Gary Player. Todo ello forma un conjunto que presta las mejores condiciones para el "dolce far niente".

Vivere e giocare a golf come un barone italiano? L'atmosfera di Palazzo Arzaga, di proprietà dell'omonima famiglia, nelle vicinanze del lago di Garda, sembra fatta apposta. L'hotel di prima categoria, con la spa e il resort golfistico, unisce in modo affascinante tradizione e modernità. Le sale del palazzo del 15° secolo – contenente ancora in parte affreschi risalenti a quell'epoca – sono arredate con mobili antichi e dispongono nello stesso tempo di TV satellitare e connessione ISDN. I due campi da golf sono stati realizzati da Jack Nicklaus II e Gary Player, professionisti di indiscusso valore in questo settore. Tutto ciò costituisce i presupposti ideali per un raffinato "dolce far niente".

The stately private home treats guests to fabulous views inside and out—it opened its doors to hotel guests in 1999.

Herrliche Ein- und Ausblicke beschert der stattliche Privatbesitz, der 1999 seine Pforten für Hotelgäste öffnete.

Cette imposante demeure qui a ouvert ses portes aux clients en 1999 offre de toutes parts une magnifique perspective.

Magníficas vistas interiores y exteriores de una soberbia propiedad privada que abrió sus puertas a los primeros huéspedes en 1999.

L'imponente tenuta privata, che ha aperto le sue porte agli ospiti nel 1999, regala splendidi scorci sia all'interno sia all'esterno.

The estate consists of three buildings: the palazzo and the 15th century Residenza San Martino, as well as the Residenza dei Castagni with a magnificent view over the 18-hole golf course.

Die Anlage besteht aus drei Gebäuden: dem Palazzo und der Residenz San Martino aus dem 15. Jahrhundert sowie der Residenza dei Castagni mit herrlichem Blick über die 18-Loch-Anlage.

Le complexe est composé de trois bâtiments : le palais, la Résidence San Martino du 15ème siècle et la Résidence des Castagni qui offrent une vue magnifique sur le 18-trous.

El recinto cuenta con tres edificios: el palazzo y la Residenza San Martino del siglo XV, y la Residenza dei Castagni con una fantástica vista al campo de 18 hoyos.

La struttura è composta di tre edifici: il palazzo e la Residenza San Martino del 15° secolo, nonché la Residenza dei Castagni, con splendida vista sul percorso a 18 buche.

Palazzo Arzaga Hotel Spa & Golf Resort *Lake Garda, Italy*

Four Seasons Resort Provence at Terre Blanche

Tourrettes, France

The founder of SAP, Dietmar Hopp, fulfilled a dream in Provence: he created a de luxe golf resort with two 18-hole Masters courses and a five-star hotel. The hotel's main building has a total of 115 suites, built in Provençale style and each with a private terrace, which offers open views over a landscape with gorse bushes, lavender fields and oak forests, as far as the Maritime Alps. A spa and a fitness center take care of guests' physical well-being. With such a high standard, it's hardly surprising that the Faventia Restaurant was also already awarded a Michelin star.

SAP-Gründer Dietmar Hopp hat sich in der Provence einen Traum erfüllt: Ein Golf Resort der Extraklasse mit zwei 18-Loch-Meisterschaftsplätzen und einem 5-Sterne-Hotel. Ein Hauptgebäude mit insgesamt 115 Suiten, gebaut im provenzalischem Stil, mit jeweils eigener Terrasse, die Blicke freigibt auf eine Landschaft mit Ginsterbüschen, Lavendelfeldern und Eichenwäldern, bis zu den maritimen Alpen. Ein Spa und ein Fitnesscenter sorgen für körperliches Wohlbefinden. Bei solch einem hohen Standard wundert es kaum noch, dass auch das Restaurant Faventia bereits die Auszeichnung mit einem Michelin Stern erhielt.

Le fondateur de la société SAP, Dietmar Hopp, a réalisé un de ses rêves : un golf resort de luxe avec deux parcours de championnat de 18 trous et un hôtel cinq étoiles. Un bâtiment principal avec 115 suites, de style provençal avec terrasse privée dégageant la vue sur un paysage de genêts, de champs de lavande et de forêts de chêne jusqu'aux Alpes maritimes. Une villa Spa et une villa Fitness assurent le bien-être corporel. Avec une telle exclusivité, il n'est pas étonnant que le restaurant Faventia se soit déjà vu décerner une étoile par le Michelin.

Es el sueño hecho realidad del fundador de SAP, Dietmar Hopp. Un Golf Resort de alta categoría con dos campos de competición de 18 hoyos y un hotel de cinco estrellas en la Provenza. El edificio principal cuenta con 115 suites de estilo provenzal con terraza propia, y unas vistas que alcanzan hasta los Alpes Marítimos, entre paisajes de campos de retama, lavanda y robledales. Del bienestar físico se encargan el Spa y el gimnasio. Ante semejante nivel de exigencia no es de extrañar que su restaurante, Faventia, ya tenga en su poder una estrella Michelín.

Dietmar Hopp, il fondatore della SAP, ha realizzato un suo sogno in Provenza: un resort golfistico di primissimo livello con due campi da campionato a 18 buche e un hotel a 5 stelle. Un edificio principale con 115 suite, costruiti in stile provenzale, ognuno con terrazza propria, da cui lo sguardo vaga su un paesaggio fatto di cespugli di ginestre, di campi di lavanda e di querceti, fino alle Alpi marittime. Una spa ed un centro fitness assicurano il benessere fisico. Con uno standard del genere, non sorprende che anche il ristorante Faventia abbia già ricevuto in premio una stella Michelin.

The golf courses nestle in the soft, southern Provençale hills. The pool facility is uniquely positioned with a panoramic view of the surrounding countryside. The 162 m² of the spa villa also take care of guests' well-being.

Die Golfplätze schmiegen sich in die sanften, südprovenzalischen Hügel. Einmalig platziert ist die Poolanlage mit Panoramablick auf die umliegende Landschaft. Auch die 162 m² große Spa-Villa sorgt für Wohlbefinden.

Les terrains de golf s'adossent aux coteaux du sud de la Provence. La piscine offre un point de vue unique sur les paysages environnants. La villa Spa de 162 m² invite également à la relaxation.

Los campos de golf se ensamblan entre las suaves colinas del sur de Provenza. La piscina disfruta de una ubicación exclusiva con vistas panorámicas al paisaje que la rodea. La villa Spa de 162 m² es una fuente más de bienestar.

Le dolci colline della Provenza meridionale accolgono i campi da golf. La piscina ha una posizione incantevole con vista panoramica sul paesaggio circostante. Anche la villa spa, su un'area di 162 m², contribuisce al benessere degli ospiti.

110   Four Seasons Resort Provence at Terre Blanche   *Tourrettes, France*

Stone and *wood dominate the architecture, which is typical for Provence. The elegant interior shows the close relationship to the sophisticated Côte d'Azur.*

In der *Architektur dominieren Stein und Holz, die typischen Materialien für die Provence. Die elegante Einrichtung vermittelt die Nähe zur mondänen Côte d'Azur.*

L'architecture est *dominée par la pierre et le bois, matériaux typiquement provençaux. L'élégante décoration rappelle que la mondaine Côte d'Azur n'est pas loin.*

La arquitectura *se deja llevar por el estilo típico de Provenza: la madera y la piedra. La elegante decoración da un toque de proximidad al carácter mundano de la Costa Azul.*

Nell'architettura *prevalgono la pietra ed il legno, tipici della Provenza. L'eleganza dell'arredamento ricorda il sapore mondano della vicina Costa Azzurra.*

Evian Royal Resort

Evian-les-Bains, France

Framed by the French Alps, one of Europe's most exclusive hotels sits majestically in the middle of a 47 acres park above Lake Geneva. The hotel was built in the Belle Époque,—the colonnades, rotunda and frescoes are a reminder of this. But of course, the Evian Royal Resort has continually adapted to the Zeitgeist and the demands of its pampered clientele and it offers every modern comfort you can imagine. The Evian Masters takes place every year on the magnificent golf course.

Eingerahmt von den französischen Alpen, thront eines der exklusivsten Hotels Europas inmitten eines 19 Hektar großen Parks über dem Genfer See. Erbaut wurde es während der Belle Époque, an die Säulengänge, Rotunden und Fresken erinnern. Doch natürlich hat sich das Evian Royal Resort immer wieder dem Zeitgeist und dem Anspruch seiner verwöhnten Klientel angepasst und bietet jeden erdenklichen, modernen Komfort. Auf dem herrlichen Golfplatz werden jährlich die Evian Masters ausgetragen.

Enchâssé dans les Alpes françaises, l'un des hôtels les plus exclusifs d'Europe trône au cœur d'un parc de 19 hectares en surplomb du Lac de Genève. Il a été construit à la Belle Époque, ce que rappellent les colonnades, les rotondes et les fresques. Pourtant l'Evian Royal Resort ayant toujours su s'adapter à l'esprit du temps et aux exigences de sa clientèle exigeante, à laquelle il propose tout le confort moderne possible. L'Evian Masters se déroulent tous les ans sur son parcours de golf.

Enmarcado por los Alpes franceses, en un parque de 19 hectáreas sobre el Lago Léman se levanta imponente uno de los hoteles más exclusivos de Europa. Fue construido durante una Belle Époque que aún evocan sus columnatas, rotondas y frescos. Sin duda el Evian Royal Resort ha sabido siempre adaptarse al espíritu de las exigencias de su mimada clientela, ofreciendo todo el confort moderno posible. El fabuloso campo de golf es escenario anual del Evian Masters.

Nella cornice delle Alpi francesi, uno degli hotel più esclusivi d'Europa è situato al centro di un parco di 19 ettari sul lago di Ginevra. Fu costruito durante la Belle Époque, di cui sono testimonianza i colonnati, le rotonde e gli affreschi. Però, naturalmente, il Evian Royal Resort si è sempre adattato allo spirito e ai desideri della propria esigente clientela, ed offre qualsiasi tipo di comfort moderno. Lo splendido campo da golf ospita ogni anno gli Evian Master.

In addition to the golf course, the fitness center is especially attractive here. It includes a "Better Living Institute", which is regarded as one of the best spas in Europe.

Neben dem Golfplatz glänzt hier vor allem das Wellnesszentrum mit seinem „Better Living Institute", das als eines der besten Spas in Europa gilt.

À côté du golf c'est le centre de remise en forme avec son « Better Living Institute » qui resplendit. Il est considéré comme l'un des meilleurs spas en Europe.

Junto al campo de golf muestra su esplendor el centro Wellness y su "Better Living Institute", considerado uno de los mejores Spa de Europa.

Accanto al campo da golf, spicca qui soprattutto il centro wellness con il "Better Living Institute", una delle migliori spa d'Europa.

First a round of golf, then relaxing in the pool, which seems to merge with Lake Geneva, or winding down in the spa or French bed.

Erst eine Runde Golf, dann relaxen am Pool, der mit dem Genfer See zu verschmelzen scheint, im Spa oder im Französischen Bett.

Tout d'abord une partie de golf, se relaxer ensuite au bord de la piscine qui semble de fondre dans le Lac Léman, dans le spa ou dans un lit français.

Tras un tour de golf se encuentra el relax en el agua de una piscina que parece fundirse con el Lago Léman o en el Spa, descansando en el dormitorio.

Una partita a golf, poi relax in una piscina che sembra fondersi con il Lago di Ginevra, nella spa o in un ampio letto francese.

Rio Real Golf Hotel

Marbella, Spain

In a green valley only three miles from Marbella's bustling hive of activity, there is an oasis of relaxation. The 18-hole links golf course with views over the Mediterranean was already established in 1965 and in 2001 a hotel was added. The hotel was named after the river, which crosses the site and the famous interior designer Pascua Ortega furnished it. He designed the lobby, bar, restaurant and the 30 rooms and suites in a fresh and airy Mediterranean style and as a place where you can enjoy the lightness of being.

Nur fünf Kilometer vom geschäftigen Treiben Marbellas entfernt, liegt in einem grünen Tal eine Oase der Entspannung. Bereits 1965 wurde der 18-Loch-Golfplatz mit Blick auf das Mittelmeer angelegt, 2001 gesellte sich ein Hotel dazu. Es wurde benannt nach dem Fluss, der das Gelände durchkreuzt und eingerichtet von dem bekannten Innenarchitekten Pascua Ortega. Er gestaltete Lobby, Bar, Restaurant und die 30 Zimmer und Suiten frisch und luftig im mediterranen Stil, als einen Ort, an dem man die Leichtigkeit des Seins genießen kann.

À seulement cinq kilomètres de l'agitation fébrile de Marbella s'étend une oasis de calme dans une vallée verdoyante. Le 18-trous avec vue sur la méditerranée a été ouvert dès 1965; en 2001 s'y est ajouté un hôtel. La rivière Real qui traverse le parcours a donné son nom à l'hôtel décoré par le célèbre architecte d'intérieur Pascua Ortega. Il a fait du lobby, du bar, du restaurant et des 30 chambres et suites, clairs et aérés dans le style méditerranéen, des endroits où l'on savoure la légèreté de l'être.

A sólo cinco kilómetros del ajetreo de Marbella se encuentra un oasis de tranquilidad sobre un verde valle. En 1965 fue creado un campo de golf de 28 hoyos con vistas al mar, al que posteriormente, en 2001, acompañaría un hotel. Su nombre se lo debe al río que atraviesa la propiedad y su decoración al conocido diseñador de interiores Pascua Ortega. Por él han sido concebidos vestíbulo, bar y restaurante además de las 30 habitaciones y suites, en un estilo mediterráneo fresco y vaporoso, creando así un lugar que incita a gozar de la levedad del ser.

A soli cinque chilometri dal via vai di Marbella, in una verde vallata si trova un'oasi di relax. Il campo da golf a 18 buche con vista sul Mare Mediterraneo è stato realizzato già nel 1965; nel 2001 è stato aggiunto l'hotel, che prende il nome dal fiume che attraversa l'area circostante. Il noto architetto di interni, Pascua Ortega, a arredato l'interio: la lobby, il bar, il ristorante e le 30 camere e suite sono in stile mediterraneo, fresco e arioso, tipico di un posto in cui è possibile godere la leggerezza dell'essere.

An economic use of colors and decorative objets d'art show a perfect sense of style. The pool's clear-cut design invites everyone who likes swimming straight lengths.

Sparsam eingesetzte Farben und dekorative Kunstobjekte zeugen von perfektem Stilgefühl. Eine Einladung an alle, die gerne gerade Bahnen schwimmen wollen, ist der schnörkellose Pool.

Economie des couleurs et objets d'art décoratifs témoignent d'un goût parfait. La piscine, sans fioriture, est une invitation à tous ceux qui veulent faire des longueurs.

Los colores sin excesos y los objetos de arte que decoran el lugar son muestra de un perfecto sentido del estilo. La sobria piscina invita a hacer unos largos.

L'uso spartano dei colori e gli oggetti d'arte ornamentali testimoniano il perfetto senso dello stile. Un invito per tutti coloro che nuotano volentieri in vasche diritte è la piscina dalle linee semplici.

Make your putts first, then relax—in the lounge, in one of the 16 guest rooms or even in one of the eight suites, two of them measuring over 119 square yard.

Erst einlochen, dann relaxen. In der Lounge, einem der 16 Gästezimmer oder auch in einer der acht Suiten, von denen zwei über 100 m² groß sind.

D'abord une partie de golf, ensuite la détente. Dans le salon, dans l'une des 16 chambres d'hôtes ou l'une des huit suites, dont deux font plus de 100 m².

Tras los hoyos viene la relajación, ya sea en el salón, en una de las 16 habitaciones o bien de las ocho suites, dos de las cuales ocupan 100 m².

Prima mettere in buca, poi rilassarsi nella lounge, in una delle 16 camere per gli ospiti o in una delle otto suite, due delle quali superano i 100 m².

Rio Real Golf Hotel *Marbella, Spain*

Villa Padierna

Marbella, Spain

The name sounds Italian, the interior suggests a Tuscan influence. But the Villa Padierna is located in Spain—and to be precise—between Marbella and Estepona, nestling in a landscape that is rich in different varieties of flora. Oranges, olive, pomegranates, pines, cypresses and Jacaranda trees grow here. The 27 holes of the Flamingo Golf Club are named after them. But the variety of the vegetation would be enough to name another 36 golf holes. Actually, these are already being planned.

Der Name klingt italienisch, das Interieur zeigt toskanische Akzente. Die Villa Padierna liegt jedoch in Spanien und zwar genau zwischen Marbella und Estepona, eingebettet in eine Landschaft mit artenreicher Flora. Orangen, Oliven, Granatäpfel, Pinien, Zypressen und Palisander wachsen hier. Nach ihnen sind die 27 Löcher des Flamingo Golf Clubs benannt. Die Vielfalt der Vegetation würde jedoch ausreichen, um 36 weitere Golflöcher zu benennen, und tatsächlich sind sie schon geplant.

Le nom a une consonance italienne, l'intérieur porte une influence toscane. Pourtant la villa Padierna est en Espagne, exactement entre Marbella et Estepona, nichée dans un paysage riche d'une flore très diversifiée. Ici poussent orangers, oliviers, grenadiers, pins, cyprès et jacarandas. Ces arbres-mêmes mettent en valeur les 27 trous du Flamingo Golf Club. La végétation est si diversifiée qu'elle suffirait encore à dénommer les 36 trous qui sont effectivement en projet.

El nombre suena italiano y el interior evoca la Toscana. Sin embargo Villa Padierna está ubicada en España, entre Marbella y Estepona, inmersa en un paisaje de vegetación exuberante, con naranjos, olivos, granados, pinos, cipreses y jacarandá. Los 27 hoyos del campo del Flamingo Golf Club llevan sus nombres. Bien es cierto que hay vegetación suficiente para dar nombre a un campo de 36 hoyos, que incluso ya está en proyecto.

Il nome ha un suono italiano, gli interni ricordano la Toscana. Ma Villa Padierna si trova in Spagna, esattamente tra Marbella ed Estepona, adagiata in un paesaggio disseminato di fiori di ogni specie. Qui crescono arance, olive, melograni, pini, cipressi e jacarandas, che danno il nome alle 27 buche del Flamingo Golf Club. La varietà della vegetazione basterebbe tuttavia a dare il nome ad altre 36 buche, in realtà già pianificate.

Villa Padierna is located in stately fashion on a hill, with the backdrop of the Sierra Bemeja on the horizon.

Hochherrschaftlich thront die Villa Padierna auf einer Anhöhe, mit der Kulisse der Sierra Bemeja am Horizont.

La villa Padierna trône somptueusement sur une hauteur avec la Sierra Bemeja au loin en toile de fond.

La Villa Padierna se levanta imponente con la Sierra Bermeja como horizonte.

Splendidamente signorile, Villa Padierna domina da un'altura con lo sfondo della Sierra Bemeja all'orizzorte.

83 rooms and 30 suites are distributed over the hotel's different floors; and they treat guests to wonderful views of the sub-tropical environment in the south of Spain.

83 Zimmer und 30 Suiten verteilen sich auf die Etagen des Hauses, und alle bieten wunderbare Ausblicke auf die subtropische Umgebung im Süden Spaniens.

83 chambres et 30 suites se répartissent sur plusieurs étages et offrent toutes une vue superbe sur l'environnement subtropical du sud de l'Espagne.

El edificio de varias plantas alberga 83 habitaciones y 30 suites, todas ellas dotadas de vistas magníficas a este entorno subtropical del sur de España.

83 camere e 30 suite sono distribuite sui vari piani dell'edificio; tutte offrono meravigliosi scorci sul paesaggio subtropicale del sud della Spagna.

122 Villa Padierna *Marbella, Spain*

Kempinski Hotel Bahía Estepona
Estepona, Spain

The airy hotel foyer with bright frescoes and wall murals spreads a cheerful and light-hearted atmosphere. Guests look through tall glass windows into a luscious garden with generous pool facilities. The "Polly Mar Wellness and Beauty Spa" and 148 elegantly furnished rooms and suites with style influences from Africa and nautical elements also contribute to guests' well-being. Golfers take pleasure in over more than 40 extraordinary courses located nearby, including the famous Valderrama Club, the venue of the 1997 Ryder Cup.

Die luftige Hotelhalle, mit bunten Kuppelfresken und Wandbildern, verbreitet eine Atmosphäre von fröhlicher Unbeschwertheit. Durch hohe Glasfenster blickt man in einen üppigen Garten mit großzügiger Poollandschaft. Zum weiteren Wohlbefinden tragen das „Polly Mar Wellness and Beauty Spa" und 148 elegant ausgestattete Zimmer und Suiten mit afrikanischen und maritimen Stilelementen bei. Golfspieler freuen sich über mehr als 40 außergewöhnliche Golfplätze in der näheren Umgebung, darunter der berühmte Valderrama Club, wo 1997 der Ryder Cup stattgefunden hat.

Le hall de réception aérien, avec des fresques colorées et des peintures murales, répand une atmosphère de joyeuse insouciance. Grâce à de hautes baies vitrées on peut admirer un luxuriant jardin avec une grande piscine. Contribuent également au bien-être le « Polly Mar Wellness and Beauty Spa » ainsi que 148 chambres et suites élégamment aménagées avec des éléments de style africain et maritime. Les golfeurs apprécieront plus de 40 terrains de golf exceptionnels dans les environs immédiats, dont le célèbre Valderrama Club où s'est déroulée la Ryder Cup en 1997.

El espacioso vestíbulo del hotel está salpicado de frescos y pinturas murales que transmiten una atmósfera de despreocupación. Los grandes ventanales abren la vista hacia el exuberante jardín y la vasta piscina. Aún también contribuyen al bienestar el "Polly Mar Wellness and Beauty Spa" y las 148 habitaciones y suites elegantemente decoradas con detalles de África y del mar. Los amantes del golf disfrutarán de los más de 40 singulares campos ubicados en los alrededores, entre ellos el famoso Club de Golf Valderrama, que en 1997 albergó a la Ryder Cup.

L'ariosa hall dell'hotel, dalle volte vivacemente affrescate, con quadri alle pareti, trasmette un'atmosfera di allegra spensieratezza. Alte vetrate si aprono sul lussureggiante giardino e sulle piscine. Al benessere degli ospiti contribuiscono anche il "Polly Mar Wellness and Beauty Spa" e 148 camere e suite, elegantemente arredate con motivi ed elementi che ricordano l'Africa e il mare. I giocatori di golf hanno a disposizione più di 40 magnifici campi nelle immediate vicinanze, tra cui il celebre Club Valderrama, che ha ospitato il Ryder Cup nel 1997.

The magic of the palm garden is mirrored in the frescoes and pictures.

Der Zauber des Palmengartens spiegelt sich in Deckenmalereien und Bildern wider.

La magie de la palmeraie se reflète dans les peintures des plafonds et les tableaux.

La magia del jardín de palmeras se refleja en las pinturas murales y los cuadros.

La magìa del palmeto si rispecchia nei dipinti sul soffitto e nei quadri.

126 Kempinski Hotel Bahía Estepona *Estepona, Spain*

All rooms offer beach views; in fine weather, you can even see as far as Gibraltar and the African coast.

Aus allen Räumen bieten sich Blicke bis zum Strand, bei klarem Wetter sogar bis nach Gibraltar und zur afrikanischen Küste.

Toutes les chambres offrent un panorama splendide sur la plage et, par temps clair, jusqu'à Gibraltar et la côte africaine.

Todas las estancias tienen vistas a la playa, que en condiciones atmosféricas apropiadas abarcan incluso hasta Gibraltar y la costa africana.

Da tutte le sale la vista spazia fino alla spiaggia. Se il tempo lo permette, si possono scorgere addirittura Gibilterra e la costa africana.

Kempinski Hotel Bahía Estepona *Estepona, Spain*

Denia Marriott La Sella Golf Resort & Spa

Denia, Spain

The facility is located in the immediate vicinity of La Sella golf course, designed by Jose Maria Olazabal. But not only sports's enthusiasts enjoy staying here. A holistic spa is also part of the resort and offers a variety of beneficial practices for all the senses. Nature lovers soak up the beautiful countryside that stretches before the 178 rooms and eight suites. Gourmets dine to their satisfaction in the restaurant serving tasty Mediterranean dishes.

Die Anlage liegt in direkter Nachbarschaft des von Jose Maria Olazabal entworfenen Golfplatzes La Sella. Doch nicht nur Sportbegeisterte fühlen sich hier wohl. Zum Resort gehört ein ganzheitliches Spa mit einer Vielzahl wohltuender Anwendungen für alle Sinne. Naturfreunde ergötzen sich an der schönen Landschaft, die sich vor den 178 Zimmern und acht Suiten ausbreitet. Gourmets kommen im Restaurant mit den leckeren Mittelmeer-Speisen auf ihre Kosten.

Le complexe se trouve dans le voisinage du terrain de golf La Sella dessiné par José Maria Olazabal. Mais il n'y a pas que les sportifs à se sentir bien ici. Le resort comprend un spa holistique avec un grand nombre de soins bénéfiques pour tous les sens. Les amoureux de la nature se délectent du magnifique paysage qui s'étend sous les fenêtres des 178 chambres et huit suites. Les gourmets se régalent des délicieux plats méditerranéens servis par le restaurant.

La propiedad limita con el campo de golf La Sella, proyectado por José María Olazábal; aquí el placer no es sólo para los amantes del deporte, ya que el resort cuenta con un centro Spa holístico con una amplia gama de tratamientos para el deleite de los sentidos. Los amantes de la naturaleza gozarán del bello paisaje que se divisa desde las 178 habitaciones y las 8 suites. Y a los gourmets les espera un restaurante con exquisitos platos mediterráneos.

La struttura si trova nelle dirette vicinanze del campo da golf La Sella, progettato da Jose Maria Olazabal. Ma qui non si trovano a proprio agio soltanto gli appassionati di golf: del resort fa parte una spa olistica che offre una quantità di piacevoli applicazioni per il benessere di tutti i sensi. Gli amici della natura saranno rallegrati dal bel paesaggio che si stende davanti alle 178 camere e alle otto suite, mentre i buongustai saranno lieti di assaggiare nel ristorante le specialità tipiche del Mediterraneo.

The spacious, rolling pool fits into the corner of both wings of the building like a diagonal and in that way faultlessly connects interior and exterior areas.

Wie eine Diagonale fügt sich der große, geschwungene Pool in den Winkel der beiden Gebäudeflügel und verbindet damit nahtlos die Innen- und Außenbereiche.

Telle une diagonale la grande piscine en arc s'emboîte dans le coin des deux ailes du bâtiment, reliant ainsi sans obstacle les parties intérieures et extérieures.

La amplia piscina de formas curvadas se abre camino entre todos los rincones de las alas del edificio uniendo suavemente y sin cesuras los interiores y los exteriores.

La grande, sinuosa piscina si staglia come una diagonale nell'angolo formato dalle due ali dell'edificio, collegando in un tutt'uno le aree interne e quelle esterne.

Guests find two restaurants and the La Sella Spa in addition to the 18-hole golf course.

Neben dem 18-Loch-Golfplatz stehen den Gästen zwei Restaurants und das La Sella Spa zur Verfügung.

Outre le parcours de 18 trous, les hôtes bénéficient de deux restaurants et du Spa la Sella.

Además de un campo de 18 hoyos, los huéspedes disfrutarán de dos restaurantes y del Spa La Sella.

Oltre al campo da golf a 18 buche, gli ospiti hanno a disposizione due ristoranti e la Spa La Sella.

Denia Marriott La Sella Golf Resort & Spa *Denia, Spain*

Hyatt Regency La Manga
Murcia, Spain

The La Manga Club is in a favorable location. It's larger than Monaco and stretches from the Mediterranean to the Mar Menor. The Hyatt Regency La Manga Hotel is at the heart of the estate. It's impressive due to its classical architecture and quality, which is even fit for royal guests. From the roof terrace, you overlook some of the 54 holes, which make the resort so attractive for golfers. They were already the venue for the Spanish Open on several occasions. The German golf team likes to use the facility as a training ground and the spacious spa to relax the muscles.

In privilegierter Lage und größer als Monaco, erstreckt sich der La Manga Club zwischen dem Mittelmeer und dem Mar Menor. In seinem Herzen liegt das Hyatt Regency La Manga Hotel. Es besticht durch klassische Architektur und Qualität, die selbst königlichen Gästen gerecht wird. Von der Dachterrasse überblickt man einige der 54 Löcher, die das Resort so anziehend für Golfer machen und das bereits mehrere Male Austragungsort der Spanish Open war. Das deutsche Golf Team nutzt die Anlage gerne als Trainingsstützpunkt und das großzügige Spa zur Lockerung der Muskeln.

Jouissant d'une situation privilégiée entre la Méditerranée et la Mar Menor, le La Manga Club s'étend sur un espace plus grand que Monaco. En son centre se dresse l'hôtel Hyatt Regency La Manga. Il se distingue par son architecture classique et la qualité de son service satisfaisant même des désirs royaux. De la terrasse sur le toit on embrasse du regard quelques uns des 54 trous qui rendent le resort si attrayant pour les golfeurs et où s'est déjà déroulé à plusieurs reprises le Spanish Open. L'équipe de golf allemande utilise volontiers le resort comme base d'entraînement et le spa pour l'assouplissement des muscles.

En una situación privilegiada, franqueado por el Mediterráneo y el Mar Menor, está ubicado el Club La Manga, ocupando una extensión mayor que Mónaco. En su interior alberga el hotel Hyatt Regency La Manga. Su arquitectura clásica y nivel de calidad cautivan incluso a huéspedes de sangre azul. Desde la terraza de la azotea se divisa parte de los 54 hoyos, que hacen del resort un foco de atracción para golfistas y que en más de una ocasión han recibido al Spanish Open. El Golf Team alemano suele hacer buen uso del campo como apoyo para sus entrenamientos y del Spa para relajar los músculos.

In posizione privilegiata e di dimensioni maggiori di quelle del Principato di Monaco, il Club La Manga si allunga tra il Mar Mediterraneo e il Mar Menor. Al suo centro si trova l'hotel Hyatt Regency La Manga, che colpisce per la sua architettura classica e per la qualità, degna di ospiti reali. Dall'attico sono visibili alcune delle 54 buche che costituiscono l'attrazione principale dei giocatori di golf: il resort ha già ospitato più volte gli Open spagnoli. La squadra di golf tedesca utilizza volentieri sia la struttura come punto di base per gli allenamenti, sia la spaziosa spa per sciogliere i muscoli.

The colors white and cream emphasize the style of the Mediterranean buildings.

Die Farben Weiß und Creme unterstreichen den Stil der mediterranen Gebäude.

Les tons blanc et crème soulignent le style du bâtiment mediterranéen.

El estilo mediterraneo del edificio se acentúa con tonos blancos y crema.

Colori come il bianco e la crema sottolineano lo stile dell'edificio mediterraneo.

Most of the 189 rooms and suites offer a view of the golf course. After a round of golf, you can meet up in the piano bar.

Die meisten der 189 Zimmer und Suiten bieten eine Aussicht auf den Golfplatz. Nach der Runde trifft man sich in der Pianobar.

La plupart des 189 chambres et suites donnent sur le terrain de golf. Après la partie on se rencontre au pianobar.

La mayor parte de las 189 habitaciones y suites cuentan con vistas al recorrido. El pianobar es punto de encuentro tras un rato de golf.

La maggior parte delle 189 camere e suite dispongono di vista sul campo da golf. Dopo la partita, ci si incontra al pianobar.

Hyatt Regency La Manga *Murcia, Spain* 135

San Roque Club

Cádiz, Spain

Bull-fighting and the Flamenco originate from Andalusia. Tapas come from Seville and sherry was first produced in Jerez. But the famous Domecq sherry dynasty thought it was fashionable to live near Gibraltar. Today, their estate is home to the famous San Roque Golf Club, a well-known riding school and luxury hotel. Here, the guests are welcomed in true Spanish grandeur and treated to excellent service. The cuisine is highly recommended: Andalusian dishes are served in the "Bolero", whilst the "Kamakura" is possibly the best Japanese restaurant in the whole of Spain.

In Andalusien haben der Stierkampf und der Flamenco ihren Ursprung. Aus Sevilla stammen die Tapas und in Jerez wurde zum ersten Mal Sherry produziert. Die bekannte Domecq Sherry Dynastie fand es jedoch schick, in der Nähe von Gibraltar zu wohnen. Heute beherbergt ihr Anwesen den berühmten San Roque Golf Club, eine anerkannte Reitschule und ein Luxushotel. Hier werden Gäste mit spanischer Grandezza empfangen und exzellentem Service verwöhnt. Herausragend ist die Küche: Im „Bolero" werden andalusische Speisen serviert, während das „Kamakura" vielleicht das beste japanische Restaurant in ganz Spanien ist.

La tauromachie et le flamenco sont originaires d'Andalousie. Les tapas viennent de Séville et le premier vin de Xérès fut produit à Jerez. Pourtant la dynastie des Domecq, connue dans le monde entier, trouvait plus chic de vivre dans la région de Gibraltar. Aujourd'hui leur domaine abrite le célèbre San Roque Golf Club, une école d'équitation reconnue et un hôtel de luxe. Ici les hôtes sont reçus avec toute la grandeur espagnole et un service excellent. La cuisine l'est tout autant : le « Bolero » sert des mets andalous tandis que le « Kamakura » est peut-être le meilleur restaurant japonais de toute l'Espagne.

Andalucía es la cuna del flamenco y la corrida. Sevilla hizo sus primeras tapas y Jerez su primer fino. Y a la conocida dinastía Domecq le pareció que vivir cerca de Gibraltar tiene clase. Hoy su propiedad alberga el famoso club de golf San Roque, un centro ecuestre de renombre y un hotel de lujo. Aquí se trata a los huéspedes con aires de grandeza española y servicio excelente. La cocina da muestras de ello en su restaurantes "Bolero", que propone platos andaluces, y en el "Kamakura", probablemente el mejor restaurante japonés del país.

La corrida ed il flamenco hanno le loro origini in Andalusia. Le tapas sono originarie di Siviglia, mentre lo sherry è stato prodotto la prima volta a Jerez. Tuttavia, la nota dinastia di produttori di sherry Domecq riteneva chic abitare nei pressi di Gibilterra. Oggi, la loro tenuta ospita il celebre San Roque Golf Club, una rinomata scuola di equitazione ed un hotel di lusso che accoglie i propri ospiti con eleganza tutta spagnola ed un eccellente servizio. La cucina è di prim'ordine: al "Bolero" si servono piatti andalusi, mentre il "Kamakura" è forse il miglior ristorante giapponese di tutta la Spagna.

The former family estate nestles among the soft hills of the golf course and with 100 guest rooms; it's still small enough to maintain the desired club atmosphere.

Der ehemalige Familienlandsitz schmiegt sich zwischen die sanften Hügel des Golfplatzes und ist mit seinen 100 Gästezimmern immer noch klein genug, um die gewünschte Clubatmosphäre zu erhalten.

L'ancienne demeure familiale se dissimule entre les collines du parcours de golf et sa capacité d'accueil – 100 chambres – est encore suffisamment modeste pour préserver l'atmosphère de club souhaitée.

La antigua propiedad familiar se funde entre las ligeras colinas del campo de golf. Con sus 100 habitaciones es aún lo suficientemente reducida para mantener el clima intimista de club.

L'ex tenuta di famiglia si estende tra le dolci colline del campo di golf: con le sue 100 camere è ancora abbastanza piccola da conservare l'atmosfera da club che molti desiderano.

138 San Roque Club *Cádiz, Spain*

Since its opening in 1990 the San Roque Club counts among the most exclusive golf resorts in Europe.
Seit seiner Eröffnung 1990 zählt der San Roque Club zu den exklusivsten Golf Resorts von Europa.
Depuis son ouverture en 1990 le San Roque Club compte parmi les resorts de golf les plus exclusifs d'Europe.
Desde su apertura en 1990 el Club San Roque se considera dentro de los resorts de golf más exclusivos de Europa.
Sin dalla sua apertura nel 1990, il San Roque Club è uno dei resort golfistici più esclusivi d'Europa.

San Roque Club *Cádiz, Spain* 139

All the rooms and suites, which are spread around the bungalows and connected with each other by patios and Maurikian arcades, have a view of the pool, the two Master golf courses and the Sierra Bermeja on the horizon.

Alle Zimmer und Suiten, die sich in Bungalows verteilen und mit Patios und maurischen Arkaden miteinander verbunden sind, haben Blick auf den Pool, die beiden Meisterschaftsplätze und die Sierra Bermeja am Horizont.

Toutes les chambres et suites réparties en villas articulées autour de cours pavées et d'arcades mauresques ont vue sur la piscine, les deux parcours de championnat et les montagnes de la Sierra Bermeja.

Todas las habitaciones y suites se reparten en bungalows unidos entre sí con patios adoquinados y arcadas árabes. Todos ellos disponen de vistas a la piscina y a los dos campos de golf de campeonato, con la Sierra Bermeja como horizonte.

Tutte le camere e le suite ripartite nei bungalow e collegate le une alle altre da patii e da arcate moresche, hanno vista sulla piscina, sui due campi da golf da campionato e sulla Sierra Bermeja, che si allunga all'orizzonte.

140 San Roque Club *Cádiz, Spain*

San Roque Club *Cádiz, Spain*

ArabellaSheraton Golf Hotel Son Vida

Majorca, Spain

A first-class golfing holiday calls for a first-class hotel and first-class golf course. The ArabellaSheraton Golf Hotel Son Vida already has two private 18-hole golf courses that count amongst the most beautiful on the island: Son Vida Golf and Son Muntaner Golf. The hotel is in the style of a Spanish manor house and is situated above the island's capital, Palma, and in the elegant villa suburb of Son Vida, surrounded by a garden full of palms, carob and olive trees. The 93 rooms, 22 of them suites and a grand suite, offer a lifestyle culture with the ambiance of a Majorcan country house.

Zum First-Class-Golfurlaub gehört ein First-Class-Hotel und ein First-Class-Golfplatz. Das ArabellaSheraton Golf Hotel Son Vida verfügt gleich über zwei hauseigene 18-Loch-Golfplätze, die zu den schönsten der Insel zählen: Son Vida Golf und Son Muntaner Golf. Das Hotel im Stil spanischer Herrensitze liegt oberhalb der Inselhauptstadt Palma im noblen Villenvorort Son Vida, umgeben von einem Garten voller Palmen, Johannisbrot- und Olivenbäume. Die 93 Zimmer, davon 22 Suiten und eine Grand Suite, bieten Wohnkultur im mallorquinischen Landhausambiente.

Pour des vacances golfiques de première classe, un hôtel et un golf de première classe s'imposent. L'ArabellaSheraton Golf Hotel Son Vida possède deux parcours 18 trous qui comptent parmi les plus beaux de l'île : le Son Vida Golf et le Son Muntaner Golf. L'hôtel, un manoir de style espagnol, est situé au-dessus de la capitale de l'île, Palma, dans le quartier résidentiel Son Vida, dans un parc plantés de palmiers, de caroubiers et d'oliviers. Les 93 chambres, dont 22 suites et une grande suite, assurent un confort recherché dans une atmosphère de mas majorquin.

Evidentemente para unas vacaciones de golf de primera clase se requiere un hotel de primera clase y un campo de golf de primera clase. El ArabellaSheraton Golf Hotel Son Vida cuenta con dos campos propios de 18 hoyos, el Son Vida Golf y Son Muntaner Golf, que están considerados entre los más bellos de la isla. El hotel de estilo señorial está ubicado en la parte alta de la capital, Palma, cercano a la urbanización de lujo de Son Vida y rodeado de un jardín de palmeras, algarrobos y olivos. Las 93 habitaciones, 22 suites y la Grand Suite ofrecen el arte de vivir en el puro estilo rústico mallorquín.

Di una vacanza golfistica di prim'ordine fanno parte un hotel ed un campo da golf pure di prim'ordine. L'ArabellaSheraton Golf Hotel Son Vida dispone di ben due campi propri a 18 buche tra i più belli dell'isola: Son Vida Golf e Son Muntaner Golf. L'hotel, costruito nello stile delle residenze signorili spagnole, sorge nell'elegante quartiere di Son Vida, in posizione rialzata rispetto al capoluogo Palma, ed è circondato da un giardino in cui crescono palme, carrubi e ulivi. Le 93 camere, tra cui 22 suite ed una Grand Suite, sono arredate in stile rustico tipico di Maiorca.

After a day on the golf course or by the swimming pool, it's a pleasure to devote yourself to the delicacies in the "Plat d'Or" restaurant that has repeatedly been awarded a gourmet rating.

Nach einem Tag auf dem Golfplatz oder am Swimmingpool widmet man sich gerne den Schlemmereien im vielfach ausgezeichneten Gourmet-Restaurant „Plat d'Or".

Après une journée passée sur le golf ou au bord de la piscine, on apprécie le raffinement du restaurant gastronomique « Le Plat d'Or » ayant remporté de nombreuses distinctions.

Tras una jornada en el campo de golf o en la piscina se dejan seducir los sentidos en el exquisito restaurante para gourmets "Plat d'Or".

Dopo una giornata trascorsa sul campo da golf o in piscina, si gustano le specialità del rinomato ristorante "Plat d'Or", già insignito di vari premi.

Nestling among *fabulous nature, the golf course and the hotel with its Altira Spa are included in the best that the Balearics has to offer.*

Eingebettet in *eine herrliche Natur, gehören die Golfplätze und das Hotel mit seinem Altira Spa, mit zum Besten, was die Balearen zu bieten haben.*

Dans un *magnifique environnement, les golfs et l'hôtel avec son spa Altira font partie des meilleurs que proposent les Baléares.*

Inmersos en *una naturaleza encantadora, los campos de golf, el hotel y su Altira Spa se consideran entre los mejores que ofrecen las Baleares.*

Adagiati in *una stupenda natura, i campi da golf e l'hotel, con la Spa Altira, fanno parte del meglio che le Baleari possano offrire.*

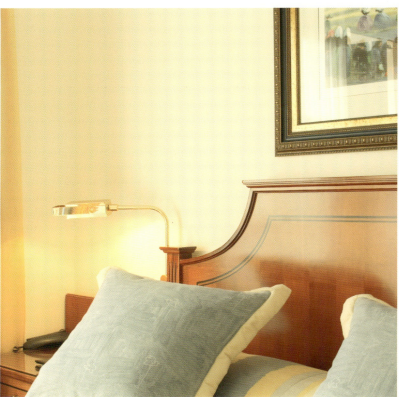

144   ArabellaSheraton Golf Hotel Son Vida   *Majorca, Spain*

ArabellaSheraton Golf Hotel Son Vida *Majorca, Spain*   145

Amanjena
Marrakech, Morocco

When the red-brown walls of this palace appear, many people perhaps think it's a mirage right in the middle of a green oasis and beneath a blue sky, in front of the white peaks of the High Atlas. The intensity of the colors is so overwhelming. A special magic floats above this peaceful paradise. Guests can relax in the hammam, enjoy a massage or simply the wonderful garden, where the scent of eucalyptus, jasmine, roses and orange blossom is in the air. Guests can dine Moroccan or Thai style and enjoy a round of golf on the neighboring Golf d'Amelkis course.

Vielleicht denkt manch einer an eine Fata Morgana, wenn vor ihm die rotbraunen Mauern dieses Palastes auftauchen, inmitten in einer grünen Oase, überspannt von blauem Himmel und vor den weißen Gipfeln des Hohen Atlas. So überwältigend ist die Intensität der Farben. Eine besondere Magie liegt über diesem friedlichen Paradies. Man entspannt im Hamam, bei Massagen oder einfach im wunderschönen Garten, wo es nach Eukalyptus, Jasmin, Rosen und Orangenblüten duftet. Man speist marokkanisch oder thailändisch und spielt eine Runde auf dem benachbarten Platz Golf d'Amelkis.

C'est presque comme un mirage de se trouver devant les murs rouge brique du palais, au cœur d'une oasis de verdure, sous le bleu du ciel et face aux sommets enneigés du Haut Atlas. L'intensité des couleurs est absolument sublime. Ce paradis paisible est empreint d'une magie particulière. On se détend au hamam, avec des massages ou tout simplement dans de somptueux jardins embaumant l'eucalyptus, le jasmin, la rose et la fleur d'oranger. On se régale de plats marocains ou thaïlandais et l'on joue une partie sur le golf d'Amelkis voisin.

En medio de un oasis envuelto por un cielo azul y los picos nevados del Alto Atlas, se vislumbran los muros rojizos de un palacio como si de un espejismo se tratase. La abrumadora intensidad de los colores llena de magia este paraíso de paz. El relax se encuentra en el Hamam, en los masajes o simplemente en el fabuloso jardín que desprende aromas de eucalipto, jazmín, rosas y azahar. Aquí se puede disfrutar de la cocina marroquí y tailandesa o hacer una ronda de golf en el vecino recorrido de Golf d'Amelkis.

Qualcuno penserà ad un miraggio, vedendo apparire le mura rossicce di questo palazzo nel mezzo di un'oasi verde, ricoperta dall'azzurro del cielo davanti alle cime candide dell'Alto Atlante. L'intensità dei colori è straordinaria. Una magìa particolare regna su questo paradiso di pace. Gli ospiti si rilassano nell'hamam, facendo massaggi, o semplicemente nel magnifico giardino, tra i profumi di eucalipto, gelsomino, rose e fiori d'arancio. La cucina è marocchina o tailandese e si può giocare sul vicino percorso golfistico d'Amelkis.

Only 40 luxurious guest-pavilions are available. They guarantee a relaxing and private atmosphere.

Gerade einmal 40 luxuriöse Gäste-Pavillons stehen zur Verfügung. Sie garantieren eine erholsame und private Atmosphäre.

Une quarantaine de luxueux pavillons hébergent les hôtes. Ils créent une atmosphère privée véritablement reposante.

Los 40 lujosos pabellones para huéspedes garantizan un ambiente de privacidad y sosiego.

Sono disponibili per gli ospiti soltanto 40 pavillon di lusso, che garantiscono un'atmosfera privata e riposante.

Shady inner *courtyards and artistic fountains offer somewhere cool before the heat of midday. At twilight, the colors of the sky and the illumination are fascinating.*

Schattige Innenhöfe *und kunstvolle Brunnen spenden Kühle vor der Hitze der Mittagsstunden. In der Dämmerung faszinieren die Farben des Himmels und der Beleuchtung.*

Des patios *ombragés et des fontaines ouvrées dispensent une fraîcheur bienvenue pendant les chaleurs de l'après-midi. Au crépuscule les couleurs du ciel et des illuminations sont fascinantes.*

Los patios *sombreados y artísticas fuentes emanan frescor en los mediodías más calurosos. Al atardecer la iluminación y los colores del cielo despiertan fascinación.*

Ombrosi cortili *interni ed artistiche fontane rinfrescano le calde ore pomeridiane. I colori del cielo e l'illuminazione donano fascino particolare al crepuscolo.*

Amanjena *Marrakech, Morocco*

The shapes *of the windows, doors and gateways are like over-sized keyholes, through which you can sneak a peek of paradise.*

Wie übergroße *Schlüssellöcher, durch die man einen Blick ins Paradies erhaschen kann, sind die Formen der Fenster, Türen und Tore.*

Semblables à *des trous de serrure démesurés, les fenêtres, portes et portails laissent entrapercevoir le paradis.*

La mirada *atraviesa las siluetas y formas de ventanas y portones que parecen enormes ojos de cerradura encerrando el paraíso.*

Le forme *delle finestre, delle porte e dei portoni ricordano quelle di gigantesche serrature attraverso le quali si può spiare il paradiso.*

Amanjena Marrakech, Morocco

Oberoi Mena House

Cairo, Egypt

This hotel is steeped in tradition and located, so to speak, in the shadow of one of the wonders of the world: the pyramids of Gizeh. It was built for the guests of honor at the inauguration of the Suez Canal in 1869. The guest book includes reigning monarchs and lots of celebrities. Agatha Christie also used to come in and out here and the suites are even named after Churchill and Montgomery. The veneer of the past gives the hotel a quite special charm, but there are also modern rooms in the new building, which is constructed in an angular shape around a garden area. For anyone who is not satisfied with the hotel's private 9-hole golf course, there are three absolutely first-rate golf courses in Cairo itself.

Dieses traditionsreiche Hotel liegt sozusagen im Schatten eines der Weltwunder, den Pyramiden von Gizeh. Erbaut wurde es für die Ehrengäste zur Einweihung des Suezkanals 1869. Von gekrönten Häuptern und viel Prominenz erzählt das Gästebuch. Auch Agatha Christie ging hier ein und aus und nach Churchill und Montgomery sind sogar Suiten benannt. Die Patina der vergangenen Jahre verleiht dem Haus einen ganz besonderen Charme, doch gibt es auch moderne Zimmer in dem Neubau, der winkelförmig um eine Gartenanlage errichtet wurde. Wem der hoteleigene 9-Loch-Golfplatz nicht genügt, findet in Kairo drei absolute Spitzenplätze.

Cet hôtel riche de traditions se situe à l'ombre d'une des merveilles du monde, les pyramides de Gizeh. Il a été construit pour loger les invités d'honneur lors de l'inauguration du canal de Suez en 1869. Le livre d'or relate la visite des têtes couronnées et des hôtes de marque. Agatha Christie fut une habituée des lieux et Churchill et Montgomery ont donné leur nom à des suites. La patine des années confère à cet hôtel un charme tout particulier, mais il y a aussi des chambres modernes dans l'aile récente construite en angle dans un parc. Le golfeur qui ne se satisfait pas du 9-trous appartenant à l'hôtel trouvera au Caire trois parcours haut de gamme.

Un hotel cargado de tradición ubicado a la sombra de una de las siete maravillas del mundo, las pirámides de Gizeh. Fue construido para alojar a los invitados de honor con motivo de la inauguración del canal de Suez en 1869. El libro de huéspedes recoge personajes famosos y de la realeza. Agatha Christie pasó aquí sus noches y tanto Churchill como Montgomery han dado nombre a suites. La pátina de años pasados transmite al lugar un encanto especial; sin embargo las habitaciones del nuevo edificio angular construido en torno a un jardín son de carácter moderno. En caso de que el campo de 9 hoyos no sea suficiente Cairo cuenta con otros tres campos de golf de élite.

Questo hotel ricco di tradizione sorge praticamente all'ombra di una delle sette meraviglie: le piramidi di Gizah. Fu costruito per gli ospiti d'onore in occasione dell'inaugurazione del Canale di Suez nel 1869. Il libro degli ospiti reca testimonianze di personaggi reali e di celebrità. Anche Agatha Christie veniva qui spesso, alcune suite portano il nome di personaggi come Churchill e Montgomery. La patina del tempo conferisce all'hotel un fascino del tutto particolare; sono disponibili però anche camere moderne nell'edificio più nuovo, costruito ad angolo intorno ad un giardino. Chi non si accontenta del campo da golf a 9 buche dell'hotel, troverà al Cairo tre campi di prim'ordine.

Guests in the Montgomery Suite, which is named after the British General, are enchanted by oriental flair. In World War Two, Montgomery put an end to the desert campaign of the Germans under General Rommel.

Orientalischer Flair verzaubert die Gäste in der Montgomery Suite, benannt nach dem britischen General, der im 2. Weltkrieg den Wüstenfeldzug der Deutschen unter General Rommel stoppte.

Un charme oriental envoûte les hôtes dans la suite Montgomery qui porte le nom du général britannique qui a stoppé la campagne du désert menée par le général allemand Rommel.

El aire oriental hechiza a los huéspedes de la suite Montgomery, cuyo nombre debe al general británico que en la II Guerra Mundial frenó la campaña en el desierto de las tropas alemanas bajo el general Rommel.

Un fascino tutto orientale strega gli ospiti della suite Montgomery, chiamata così in onore del generale britannico che nella seconda guerra mondiale fermò l'avanzata tedesca nel deserto, guidata dal generale Rommel.

Filigree woodcarvings, *wall murals that tell stories and beds with canopies seduce guests in a fairytale, Arabian world. From the balconies, the view is always of the pyramids.*

Filigrane Holzschnitzereien, *Geschichten erzählende Wandmalereien und Betten mit Baldachin, entführen die Gäste in eine märchenhafte, arabische Welt. Von den Balkonen aus blickt man stets auf die Pyramiden.*

Des sculptures *sur bois en filigrane, des peintures murales représentant des légendes et des lits à baldaquin transportent les hôtes dans la magie de l'orient. Les balcons donnent tous sur les pyramides.*

Filigranas talladas *en madera, pinturas murales que relatan historias y camas con dosel, seducen a los huéspedes trasportándoles a un mundo árabe de fábula. Los balcones muestran la ineludible vista a las pirámides.*

Legni finemente *intagliati, dipinti a muro che raccontano leggende e i letti a baldacchino rapiscono gli ospiti nel fiabesco mondo arabo. Da qualsiasi punto, dai balconi si gode la vista delle Piramidi.*

154 Oberoi Mena House *Cairo, Egypt*

Belle Mare Plage
The Resort

Poste de Flacq, Mauritius

It's not only honeymoon couples that feel like they are in paradise on Mauritius but also golfers. This especially applies to guests staying at the Hotel Belle Mare Plage. With its two Masters courses, the hotel was awarded the "Golf Resort of the Year" in 2005 and chosen out of all continents with the exception of Europe and North America. You're guaranteed an active and also relaxing holiday of the highest quality on one of the most beautiful beaches on the island. The comfortable accommodation also takes care of that—the facilities range to a presidential villa with a personal butler and private pool. There's another pampering program in the Asian-style Shiseido Pavilion. The seven restaurants offer culinary delicacies from all over the world.

Nicht nur Hochzeitspaare fühlen sich auf Mauritius wie im Paradies, sondern auch Golfer. Vor allem Gäste des Hotels Belle Mare Plage, das 2005 mit zwei Meisterschaftsplätzen zum „Golf Resort des Jahres" von allen Kontinenten, außer Europa und Nordamerika, prämiert wurde. Aktiver und gleichzeitig erholsamer Urlaub auf höchstem Niveau an einem der schönsten Strände der Insel ist gewährleistet. Dafür sorgen auch die komfortablen Unterkünfte, die bis hin zur Präsidentenvilla mit persönlichem Butler und Privatpool reichen. Ein weiteres Verwöhnprogramm gibt es im asiatisch angehauchten Shiseido Pavillon. Kulinarische Leckereien aus aller Welt bieten die sieben Restaurants.

Les jeunes mariés mais aussi les golfeurs se sentent au paradis à Maurice. Surtout les hôtes de l'hôtel Belle Mare Plage qui, avec ses deux parcours de championnat, a été couronné en 2005 « Golf Resort de l'année » de tous les continents, en dehors de l'Europe et de l'Amérique du nord. Ceci promet des vacances à la fois sportives et reposantes, dans le plus grand luxe, au bord de l'une des plus belles plages de l'île. Pour cela, plusieurs catégories de confortables villas, jusqu'à la villa présidentielle avec majordome attitré et piscine privée. Le pavillon Shiseido d'inspiration asiatique est un havre de relaxation supplémentaire. Les sept restaurants servent de délicieuses spécialités du monde entier.

Mauricio es el paraíso tanto de parejas de recién casados como de golfistas. Especialmente si se alojan en el hotel Belle Mare Plage. Construido en 2005 con dos campos de torneo, ya tiene en su haber el título de "Resort de Golf del año" de todos los continentes excepto de Europa y Norteamérica. Aquí se ofrecen vacaciones de alta calidad relajantes y activas a la vez, en una de las playas más bellas de la isla. De ello se encarga un alojamiento confortable a todos los niveles incluso, si se quiere, en villa presidencial con mayordomo y piscina propios. El Shiseido Pavillon y su aire asiático contribuyen también al relax. Los siete restaurantes seducen con sabores de todos los rincones del mundo.

Non soltanto le coppie in viaggio di nozze, ma anche i giocatori di golf si sentono in paradiso alle Mauritius. Soprattutto gli ospiti dell'hotel Belle Mare Plage, con due campi da campionato, premiato nel 2005 con il titolo di „Resort golfistico dell'anno" tra tutti i continenti, tranne Europa e Nordamerica. La struttura assicura una vacanza di altissimo livello, attiva e nello stesso tempo riposante, su una delle spiagge più belle dell'isola, a cui contribuisce anche il comfort di cui sono dotati gli alloggi: tra essi, è disponibile anche una villa presidenziale con maggiordomo personale e piscina privata. Un altro piacevole programma si svolge nel pavillon Shiseido, di carattere asiatico. Sette ristoranti offrono specialità culinarie di tutto il mondo.

The style of the Hotels Constance is visible in clear lines, refined materials and cleverly construed light sources.

Der Stil der Constance Hotels zeigt sich in klaren Linien, edlen Materialien und geschickt inszenierten Lichtquellen.

Le style des hôtels Constance est caractérisé par des lignes pures, des matériaux nobles et une adroite mise en scène des éclairages.

El estilo de los hoteles Constance está basado en líneas claras, materiales nobles y sutiles fuentes de luz.

Lo stile dell'hotel Constance si presenta con linee limpide, materiali pregiati e sorgenti di luce sapientemente distribuite.

A calm atmosphere circulates around the rooms, villas and lakes or lagoons of the world-class golf course "The Legend".

Eine ruhige Atmosphäre liegt über den Zimmern, den Villen und den Seen bzw. Lagunen des Weltklasse-Golfplatzes „The Legend".

Une atmosphère paisible règne sur les chambres, les villas et les lacs ou plutôt les lagunes du parcours de classe internationale « The Legend ».

La atmósfera de armonía se propaga a las habitaciones, las villas, y a los lagos y lagunas del elitista campo de golf "The Legend".

Un'atmosfera tranquilla regna sulle camere, le ville e sugli specchi d'acqua e le lagune del campo da golf di classe internazionale "The Legend".

Belle Mare Plage The Resort *Poste de Flacq, Mauritius*

Lémuria Resort of Praslin

Praslin, Seychelles

According to legend, Lémuria is a taste of paradise that emerged from the sea when the earth divided and pushed the continents apart. It's been untouched for many centuries. To preserve this natural quality, the resort was carefully built between the exotic jungle landscape and three dream beaches, where the tortoises continue to nest today without being disturbed. Natural materials were used for the buildings and the interior furnishing of the 96 suites, eight pool villas and a presidential villa measuring 1500 square yard. The design was adapted to nature in order to retain the extraordinary beauty of the Seychelles.

Der Legende nach ist Lémuria ein Stück vom Paradies, das aus dem Meer auftauchte, als die Erde sich teilte und die Kontinente auseinander schob. Unberührt über viele Jahrhunderte. Um diese Natürlichkeit zu erhalten, wurde das Resort behutsam zwischen die exotische Dschungellandschaft und drei Traumstrände eingefügt, wo heute noch ungestört Schildkröten nisten. Für die Gebäude und die Inneneinrichtung der 96 Suiten, acht Poolvillen und einer 1250 m² großen Präsidentenvilla wurden natürliche Materialien verwendet, das Design der Natur angepasst, um die außergewöhnliche Schönheit der Seychellen zu bewahren.

D'après la légende, Lémuria est un morceau de paradis qui surgit de la mer quand la terre se fendit et sépara les continents. Intact pendant plusieurs siècles. Pour préserver ce naturel, le resort se fond prudemment entre une jungle exotique et trois plages de rêve, où les tortues viennent encore pondre tranquillement. Pour les bâtiments et l'aménagement intérieur des 96 suites, des huit villas avec piscine privée et de la suite présidentielle d'une superficie de 1250 m², on a privilégié des matériaux naturels, en harmonie avec l'environnement, dans le respect de l'exceptionnelle beauté des Seychelles.

Cuenta la leyenda que Lémuria es un fragmento del paraíso que emergió del fondo del mar al dividirse la Tierra separando los continentes. Y así permaneció intacto durante siglos. Con el fin de preservar esa naturalidad primitiva el resort ha sido integrado cuidadosamente en un paisaje de exótica selva y tres playas de ensueño, en las que aún hoy incuban las tortugas sin sentirse perturbadas. La construcción y decoración de las 96 suites, ocho villas con piscina y la villa presidencial de 1250 m² se ha llevado a cabo con materiales naturales, adaptando el diseño al entorno y a fin de mantener intacta la incomparable belleza de las Seychelles.

La leggenda racconta che Lémuria sia un pezzo di paradiso spuntato dal mare nel momento in cui la terra si aprì separando i continenti. Per molti secoli questo posto è rimasto inviolato. Per lasciare intatta la natura del luogo, il resort è stato realizzato tra il paesaggio esotico della giungla e tre splendide spiagge, dove ancora oggi le tartarughe costruiscono indisturbate il nido. Per la costruzione degli edifici e l'arredamento degli interni delle 96 suite, delle otto ville con piscina e della villa presidenziale, grande 1250 m², sono stati utilizzati materiali e design di ispirazione naturale, allo scopo di lasciare intatta la straordinaria bellezza delle Seychellen.

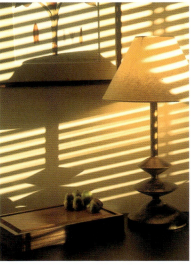

Hotel guests can enjoy a free round of golf on the golf course that borders on the fabulous bay of Anse Georgette.

Hotelgäste spielen kostenlos auf dem Golfplatz, der an die herrliche Bucht von Anse Georgette grenzt.

Les résidents de l'hôtel accèdent gratuitement au golf, longeant la magnifique baie d'Anse Georgette.

Los huéspedes del hotel disponen del uso gratuito del campo de golf, que limita con la fabulosa bahía de Anse Georgette.

Gli ospiti dell'hotel possono utilizzare gratis il campo da golf, confinante con la splendide insenatura di Anse Georgette.

A spa spoils guests with high-quality treatments; a doctor gives tips on losing weight and improving physical fitness.

Ein Spa verwöhnt mit hochwertigen Anwendungen, ein Arzt gibt Tipps zum Abnehmen und zur Förderung der körperlichen Fitness.

Un spa fait découvrir des soins haut de gamme, un médecin dispense des conseils pour maigrir et améliorer sa forme physique.

El Spa agasaja con tratamientos de alta calidad y cuenta con un asesoramiento médico para terapias de adelgazamiento y puesta en forma.

Una spa assicura il benessere con applicazioni di prim'ordine, un medico segue gli ospiti con consigli per dimagrire e per migliorare la forma fisica.

164   Lémuria Resort of Praslin   *Praslin, Seychelles*

The Western Cape Hotel & Spa
Hermanus, South Africa

The resort that belongs to the ArabellaSheraton group is located about 68 miles east from Cape Town near Hermanus, a well-known spot for whale watching. The hotel with the AltiraSPA is classically elegant and designed with African natural stones and local art; and it offers panoramic views of a nature reserve right in the middle of the largest lagoon in South Africa. The 18-hole golf course by Peter Matkovich was already nominated as South Africa's best new golf course shortly after its completion in 1999. The undulating greens count amongst the fastest in the Cape.

Das zur ArabellaSheraton Gruppe gehörende Resort liegt rund 110 Kilometer östlich von Kapstadt in der Nähe von Hermanus, einem bekannten Beobachtungsplatz für Wale. Das Hotel mit AltiraSPA ist klassisch-elegant mit afrikanischen Natursteinen und lokaler Kunst gestaltet und bietet Panoramablicke auf ein Naturreservat inmitten der größten Lagune Südafrikas. Der 18-Loch-Kurs von Peter Matkovich wurde bereits kurz nach der Fertigstellung 1999 zum besten neuen Golfplatz Südafrikas gekürt, die hügeligen Grüns zählen zu den schnellsten am Kap.

Ce resort qui appartient au groupe ArabellaSheraton est à environ 110 kilomètres à l'est de Cape Town près d'Hermanus, un point d'observation des baleines très connu. L'hôtel, doté d'un AltiraSPA, de facture classique élégante, avec de la pierre africaine naturelle et des objets d'art locaux, offre un beau panorama sur le plus grand lagon d'Afrique du Sud dans une réserve naturelle. Peu après son ouverture en 1999, le 18-trous de Peter Matkovich a été déclaré meilleur nouveau parcours d'Afrique du Sud ; ses greens vallonnés sont parmi les plus rapides du Cap.

El resort es parte del grupo ArabellaSheraton y está situado a unos 110 kilómetros al este de Ciudad del Cabo, cercano al conocido punto de observación de ballenas de Hermanus. El hotel cuenta con un AltiraSPA y está concebido en un estilo clásico y elegante salpicado de piedras naturales labradas y arte local africano. A ello se suma la magnífica vista panorámica a la reserva natural en la laguna más grande de Sudáfrica. Apenas finalizado en 1999, el recorrido de 18 hoyos de Peter Matkovich fue nombrado el mejor campo de golf nuevo del país. Sus ondulados greens se consideran de los más rápidos del Cabo.

Il resort appartenente al gruppo ArabellaSheraton si trova a circa 110 chilometri ad est di Città del Capo nei pressi di Hermanus, un noto posto di osservazione delle balene. L'hotel con AltiraSPA è in stile classico-elegante, impreziosito da pietre naturali africane e da arte locale, ed offre scorci panoramici su una riserva naturale al centro della più grande laguna sudafricana. Già subito dopo la sua realizzazione nel 1999, il percorso a 18 buche di Peter Matkovich è risultato il miglior nuovo campo da golf del Sudafrica – i suoi green ondulati sono considerati i più veloci del Capo.

The entrance hall, bathed in light, is striking for its impressive wood construction that is combined with natural stone walls.

Die lichtdurchflutete Eingangshalle besticht durch eine eindrucksvolle Holzkonstruktion in Verbindung mit Natursteinmauern.

Le hall de réception inondé de lumière éblouit par sa construction en bois impressionnante combinée avec des murs de pierre naturelle.

La vista es cautivada por la impresionante estructura en madera y paredes de piedra de un hall inundado de luz.

La luminosa hall d'ingresso spicca per una imponente costruzione in legno e per i muri in pietra naturale.

*145 **elegant** rooms in warm colors offer a view of the golf course and lagoon.*
*145 **Zimmer**, elegant und in warmen Farben, bieten Aussicht auf den Golfplatz und die Lagune.*
*145 **chambres**, élégantes, aux couleurs chaudes, offrent une jolie vue sur le golf et la lagune.*
*Las 145 **elegantes** habitaciones de tonos cálidos ofrecen vistas al campo de golf y a la laguna.*
*145 **camere**, eleganti e dai colori caldi, si affacciano sul campo da golf e sulla laguna.*

168   The Western Cape Hotel & Spa   *Hermanus, South Africa*

Zimbali Lodge
Kwa Zulu Natal, South Africa

You can do what you like here: go on safari through one of the oldest wildlife reserves in the world, sunbathe on the golden beach of the Indian Ocean or play golf on the wonderful course designed by Tom Weiskopf. Zimbali Lodge is hidden away about 25 miles north of Durban, on the Dolphin coast of Kwa Zulu Natal with a boutique hotel and various chalets, many of them located directly on the fairway. The interior of the chalets is luxurious, but in harmony with nature that begins right outside the door.

Hier kann man machen, was man will: Safari durch eines der ältesten Wildreservate der Welt, Sonnenbaden am goldenen Strand des Indischen Ozeans oder Golf spielen auf dem wunderschönen Platz von Tom Weiskopf. Die Zimbali Lodge versteckt sich rund 40 Kilometer nördlich von Durban an der Delphinküste von Kwa Zulu Natal mit einem Boutiquehotel und diversen Chalets, manche davon direkt an den Fairways. Ihr Interieur ist luxuriös, aber in Harmonie mit der Natur, die direkt vor der Tür beginnt.

Ici on peut faire ce qu'on veut : du safari dans l'une des plus anciennes réserves du monde, des bains de soleil sur la plage dorée de l'océan indien ou du golf sur le merveilleux terrain de Tom Weiskopf. Le Zimbali Lodge, planté à environ 40 kilomètres au nord de Durban sur la côte des dauphins de Kwa Zulu Natal, comprend un hôtel avec des boutiques et divers pavillons, dont certains directement au bord des fairways. Ses intérieurs sont luxueux mais en harmonie avec la nature qui s'étend à ses pieds.

Aquí se puede hacer lo que se quiera: disfrutar de un safari en una de las reservas naturales más antiguas del mundo, darse baños de sol en las doradas playas del Océano Índico o bien dedicarse a jugar al golf en el campo de Tom Weiskopf. Escondido en la costa de los delfines de Kwa Zulu Natal, a 40 kilómetros al norte de Durban, el Zimbali Lodge ofrece su Boutique hotel y varios chalés, algunos de ellos ubicados directamente en los fairways. Su interior es lujoso pero armoniza plenamente con la naturaleza que se abre a sus puertas.

Qui si può fare ciò che si vuole: il safari in una delle riserve di caccia più antiche del mondo, prendere il sole sulla spiaggia dorata dell'Oceano Indiano o giocare a golf sul magnifico campo di Tom Weiskopf. Lo Zimbali Lodge si nasconde a circa 40 chilometri a nord di Durban, sulla costa dei delfini di Kwa Zulu Natal, con un boutique hotel e diversi chalet, alcuni dei quali posizionati direttamente sui fairway. Gli interni sono di gran lusso ma in armonia con la natura che inizia direttamente sulla soglia dell'hotel.

Precious, African woods dominate in the rooms. The stone and wood construction of the buildings emanates the simplicity of Balinese architecture in terms of style.

In den Räumen dominieren edle, afrikanische Hölzer. Die Stein-Holz-Konstruktion der Gebäude ist im Stil an die Schlichtheit balinesischer Architektur angelehnt.

Dans les pièces dominent les essences africaines. Les bâtiments construits en pierre et en bois s'inspirent de la simplicité de l'architecture balinaise.

En las habitaciones destacan las maderas nobles africanas. La construcción en piedra y madera está concebida en el estilo y la austeridad de la arquitectura de Bali.

Nelle sale dominano pregiati legni africani. Lo stile degli edifici, costruiti in pietra e legno, si ispira alla semplicità dell'architettura di Bali.

The view out of the window frontage into the lobby looks directly out onto the pool, whose surface seems to merge indistinguishably with the sea.

Der Blick aus der Fensterfront der Lobby fällt direkt auf den Pool, dessen Oberfläche sich scheinbar nahtlos mit dem Meer verbindet.

De la façade vitrée du lobby, le regard plonge directement dans la piscine, dont les reflets se fondent pratiquement avec la mer.

La vista desde los ventanales del vestíbulo se abre directamente a una piscina que parece fundirse suavemente con el mar.

La vista dalla finestra frontale della Lobby dà direttamente sulla piscina, la cui superficie sembra si unisca senza soluzione di continuità a quella del mare.

Zimbali Lodge Kwa Zulu Natal, South Africa

Pezula Resort Hotel & Spa

Knysna, South Africa

You feel happy and without a care in the world surrounded by the golden beaches of the Indian Ocean, the lagoon of the pretty little town of Knysna, the impressive Outeniqua mountains and an endless blue sky above. The luxurious Pezula Resort Hotel & Spa includes 78 suites, a spa and fitness center, whisky and a cigar bar, gourmet restaurant—and as is fitting for South Africa—a well-stocked wine cellar. This facility was opened in 2005 and is still largely unknown on the international scene, even though it counts amongst Africa's most beautiful resorts.

Umrahmt von den goldenen Stränden des Indischen Ozeans, der Lagune des hübschen Städtchens Knysna, den beeindruckenden Outeniqua Bergen und einem endlos blauen Himmel darüber, fühlt man sich wunschlos glücklich. Zu dem luxuriösen Pezula Resort Hotel & Spa gehören 78 Suiten, Spa und Fitnesscenter, Whisky- und Zigarrenbar, Gourmet-Restaurant – und wie es sich für Südafrika gehört – ein gut bestückter Weinkeller. Diese 2005 eröffnete Anlage ist international noch weitgehend unbekannt, zählt jedoch zu den schönsten Resorts Afrikas.

Entouré des plages dorées de l'océan indien, de la lagune de la jolie petite ville de Knysna, des imposants Monts Outeniqua, avec un ciel infiniment bleu au-dessus de soi, on se sent parfaitement heureux. Le luxueux Pezula Resort Hotel & Spa comprend 78 suites, un spa et centre de fitness, un bar à whisky et cigares, un restaurant gastronomique et – comment pourrait-il en être autrement en Afrique du sud – une cave à vins bien approvisionnée. Ce complexe ouvert en 2005 qui est encore peu connu au plan international fait pourtant partie des plus beaux resorts d'Afrique.

Arropado por las playas del Océano Índico, la laguna de la vistosa localidad de Knysna, y las impresionantes montañas de Outeniqua uno siente la felicidad plena. Y en este escenario está ubicado el Pezula Resort Hotel & Spa, que cuenta con 78 suites, Spa y gimnasio, bar, salón de fumador, restaurante para gourmets, y una completa bodega, como es de esperar en Sudáfrica. La propiedad ha sido inaugurada en 2005 y si bien aún es poco conocida a nivel internacional ya se le considera uno de los resorts más bellos de África.

Circondati dalle spiagge dorate dell'Oceano Indiano, dalla laguna della bella cittadina di Knysna, dall'imponente catena montuosa Outeniqua, sovrastati da un infinito cielo azzurro, ci si sente assolutamente felici. Del lussuoso Pezula Resort Hotel & Spa fanno parte 78 suite, Spa e centro fitness, bar con whisky e sigari, ristorante di prim'ordine e – come di consuetudine in Sudafrica – una fornitissima cantina. Questa struttura, aperta nel 2005, internazionalmente ancora poco conosciuta, è uno dei più bei resort africani.

Warm earth colors, stone walls, lots of wood and local handicraft reflect Africa's nature.

Warme Erdfarben, Steinmauern, viel Holz und einheimisches Kunsthandwerk, spiegeln die Natur Afrikas wider.

De chaudes couleurs terre, des murs de pierre, beaucoup de bois et d'artisanat d'art local reflètent la nature africaine.

Tonos cálidos, muros de piedra, madera y artesanía que son vivo reflejo de la naturaleza de África.

I caldi colori della terra, i muri di pietra, molto legno e l'artigianato locale rispecchiano la natura dell'Africa.

The view out of the window looks out onto the golf course, whose spectacular fairways run along the cliffs by the Indian Ocean.

Der Blick aus dem Fenster geht zum Golfplatz, dessen spektakuläre Bahnen entlang der Klippen am Indischen Ozean verlaufen.

De la fenêtre, le regard tombe sur le golf, dont les fairways spectaculaires longent les rochers au bord de l'océan indien.

Las vistas abarcan un campo de golf de recorridos espectaculares a lo largo de acantilados que cortan dramáticamente el Océano Índico.

Le finestre si affacciano sul campo da golf, il cui percorso spettacolare corre lungo le scogliere dell'Oceano Indiano.

Banyan Tree Bintan

Bintan Island, Indonesia

Often, the most beautiful golf courses are hidden away on small islands. Greg Norman chose the Indonesian island of Bintan for one of his championship courses, because he found everything that makes a course interesting in this one place. Long beaches, palm groves, tropical forests, cliffs and a wind from the South China Sea. Nestled in this poetic ambiance, groups of luxurious villas, designed with every modern comfort and in typical Indonesian style, are grouped together to form the Banyan Tree Bintan. Just a short hop from Singapore one can leave the hectic world behind.

Die schönsten Golfplätze liegen oftmals versteckt auf kleinen Inseln. Greg Norman hat für einen seiner Meisterschaftsplätze das indonesische Bintan Island gewählt, weil er hier alles vorfand, was einen Platz interessant macht. Weite Strände, Palmenhaine, tropische Wälder, Felsen und der Wind vom Südchinesischen Meer. Eingebunden in dieses poetische Ambiente gruppieren sich luxuriöse Villen, eingerichtet mit allem Komfort im typisch indonesischen Stil, zum Banyan Tree Resort. Nicht weit entfernt von Singapur, kann man hier die hektische Welt weit hinter sich lassen.

Les plus beaux terrains de golf se cachent souvent sur de petites îles. Pour l'un de ses parcours de championnat, Greg Norman a sélectionné l'île indonésienne de Bintan parce qu'il y a trouvé tout ce qui rend un endroit intéressant : des plages étendues, des cocotiers, des forêts tropicales, des rochers et le vent de la mer de Chine du sud. Dans cette atmosphère poétique, de luxueuses villas de style balinais, équipées de tout le confort composent le Banyan Tree Resort. Dans ce joyau proche de Singapour, on peut laisser loin derrière soi l'agitation frénétique du monde.

Los campos de golf más hermosos se esconden con frecuencia en las islas más pequeñas. Greg Norman ha elegido esta isla de Indonesia para su recorrido de campeonato puesto que reúne todas las condiciones que hacen interesante a un lugar: vastas playas, palmerales, selva tropical, formaciones rocosas y la brisa del Mar de la China Meridional. Ensambladas en semejante ambiente idílico se ubican las lujosas villas dotadas de todo el confort y el estilo indonesio que conforman el Banyan Tree Resort. Si bien Singapur no queda lejos, la sensación de ajetreo y el estrés se esfuman al llegar al resort.

I campi da golf più belli sono spesso nascosti su piccole isole. Greg Norman ha scelto l'isola Bintan, in Indonesia, per uno dei suoi percorsi da campionato: qui ha infatti trovato tutto ciò che rende interessante un campo, dalle larghe spiagge, ai palmeti, alle foreste tropicali, alle rocce, fino al vento proveniente dal Mar Cinese Meridionale. Incastonate in questa poetica atmosfera, alcune lussuose ville, arredate con tutti i comfort in stile tipicamente indonesiano, si raggruppano nel Banyan Tree Resort. Non lontano da Singapore, è qui possibile lasciare dietro di sè il mondo e la vita frenetica.

Pure enjoyment: sunset by a private pool, dinner in one of the exquisite restaurants, dreaming in a four-poster bed.

Genuss pur: Sonnenuntergang am eigenen Pool, Dinner in einem der exquisiten Restaurants, Träume im Himmelbett.

Un plaisir sans nuage : coucher de soleil au bord de la piscine privée, dîner dans l'un des exquis restaurants, rêves dans un lit à baldaquin.

Placer en su máxima expresión: disfrutar de atardeceres desde la piscina privada, de la cena en uno de los exquisitos restaurantes y vivir los sueños en una cama con dosel.

Piacere puro: il tramonto sui bordi della propria piscina, cena in uno degli eccellenti locali, sognando in un letto baldaccino.

182 Banyan Tree Bintan *Bintan Island, Indonesia*

Exclusive lifestyle in a tropical ambiance: Spa Pool Villa, Bayfront Pool Villa or Jacuzzi Villa On-The-Rocks.
Exklusiver Lifestyle in tropischem Ambiente: Spa Pool Villa, Bayfront Pool Villa oder Jacuzzi Villa On-The-Rocks.
Lifestyle exclusif dans une ambiance tropicale : Spa Pool Villa, Bayfront Pool Villa ou Jacuzzi Villa On-The-Rocks.
Estilo de vida exclusivo en ambiente tropical: Spa Pool Villa, Bayfront Pool Villa o Jacuzzi Villa On-The-Rocks.
Stile di vita esclusivo in atmosfera tropicale: Spa Pool Villa, Bayfront Pool Villa o Jacuzzi Villa On-The-Rocks.

The Andaman

Langkawi, Malaysia

The reception lobby's extraordinary architecture is open on all sides, so that a soft breath of fresh air is always circulating through the rooms. This is a "Palace of Winds". Sunlight streams down through gables and paints enchanting reflections on the shining wooden floor. The temple-like atmosphere already makes you relax when you arrive. Then, guests occupy their luxurious rooms or their suites, which are influenced by Japanese or Malaysian elements, exactly like the four different restaurants and the lobby lounge.

Die außergewöhnliche Architektur der Empfangshalle ist nach allen Seiten offen, so dass immer ein sanfter Lufthauch durch die Räume weht. Ein „Palast der Winde". Sonnenlicht fällt durch die Giebel und malt bezaubernde Reflexe auf den glänzenden Holzboden. Die tempelartige Atmosphäre schenkt bereits bei der Ankunft Entspannung. Danach beziehen die Gäste ihre luxuriösen Zimmer oder ihre Suite, die von japanischen oder malaysischen Elementen beeinflusst sind, genau wie die vier verschiedenen Restaurants und die Lobby Lounge.

Le hall d'entrée à l'architecture exceptionnelle est ouvert de tous les côtés si bien qu'une légère brise souffle toujours dans les pièces. Un « palais des vents ». Le soleil se réfléchit à travers les frontons en un kaléidoscope de lumière sur les parquets luisants. Comme dans un temple la quiétude du lieu suscite la détente dès l'arrivée. Les hôtes rejoignent ensuite leurs luxueuses chambres ou suites décorées d'éléments d'influence malaise et japonaise que l'on retrouvent dans les quatre restaurants et le salon du hall d'entrée.

El vestíbulo goza de una arquitectura excepcional completamente abierta que deja jugar a la brisa entre las estancias, como en un verdadero "Palacio de los Vientos". La luz solar penetra por los tejados describiendo sombras cautivadoras en los pulidos suelos de madera. La atmósfera de templo envuelve y relaja nada más entrar. Tanto las lujosas habitaciones y las suites como los cuatro restaurantes y el salón del vestíbulo están decorados con elementos de influencia japonesa y malaya.

La straordinaria architettura della hall d'entrata è aperta su tutti i lati, lasciando che un leggero alito di vento spiri sempre attraverso le sale. Un "palazzo dei venti": la luce del sole filtra attraverso la cupola dipingendo magici riflessi sul lucido pavimento di legno. L'atmosfera, che ricorda quella di un tempio, dona distensione già al momento dell'arrivo. Subito dopo, gli ospiti prendono possesso delle loro lussuose camere o delle suite, arredate con elementi giapponesi o malesi, esattamente come i quattro diversi ristoranti e la Lobby Lounge.

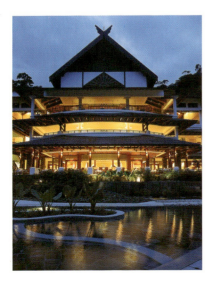

The open building style—typical for the country—with lots of wood is carried through the entire estate.

Der landestypische offene Baustil mit viel Holz zieht sich durch die gesamte Anlage.

Ce style de construction ouverte de toutes parts très typique avec beaucoup de bois se retrouve dans tout l'établissement.

Todo el complejo está caracterizado por el estilo de construcción del país, abierto y rico en madera.

Lo stile architettonico aperto, tipico del paese, con molto legno, caratterizza l'intera struttura.

The 186 rooms and suites each offer a private terrace with a view of Andaman Sea.
Die 186 Zimmer und Suiten bieten jeweils eine eigene Terrasse mit Blick auf die Andaman See.
Les 186 chambres et suites possèdent toutes leur propre terrasse avec vue sur la mer d'Andaman.
Las 186 habitaciones y suites disponen de terraza propia con vistas al Mar de Andaman.
Le 186 camere e suite dispongono ognuna di terrazza propria con vista sul mare di Andaman.

The Andaman Langkawi, Malaysia

The Datai

Langkawi, Malaysia

A luxury resort right in the middle of an intact rain forest? The architect Kerry Hill solved the problem brilliantly. The 40 villas, 54 rooms, nine suites, three restaurants, fitness center, spa and swimming pool are hardly visible, even from the fine, icing-sugar sandy beach. The buildings were integrated as carefully as possible into the original surroundings of the island of Langkawi and equipped with every comfort, with the furnishing mainly consisting of authentic materials and local handcrafted artwork.

Ein Luxus-Resort mitten im intakten Regenwald? Architekt Kerry Hill hat die Aufgabe vortrefflich gelöst. Selbst vom puderzuckerweichen Strand sind die 40 Villen, 54 Zimmer, neun Suiten, drei Restaurants, Fitnesscenter, Spa und Swimmingpool kaum zu sehen. Sie wurden so schonend wie möglich der urwüchsigen Umgebung der Insel Langkawi angepasst und mit allem Komfort ausgestattet, wobei die Einrichtung vorwiegend aus authentischen Materialien und einheimischem Kunsthandwerk besteht.

Un resort de luxe au cœur d'une forêt tropicale intacte ? L'architecte Kerry Hill a magnifiquement résolu l'équation. De la plage au sable aussi fin que du sucre en poudre on distingue à peine les 40 villas, 54 chambres, neuf suites, trois restaurants, le centre de fitness, le spa et la piscine. Tout ceci s'intègre aussi harmonieusement que possible dans la végétation tropicale primitive de l'île de Langkawi, avec tout le confort cependant. La décoration fait appel à des matériaux authentiques et des objets d'artisanat d'art local.

¿Es posible insertar un resort de lujo en plena selva virgen? El arquitecto Kerry Hill no vio ningún inconveniente en ello. Desde la playa de arena fina apenas se aprecian las 40 villas, 54 habitaciones, nueve suites, 3 restaurantes, gimnasio, piscina y Spa. Todo ello ha sido adaptado fielmente al entorno salvaje de la isla de Langkawi y dotado de pleno confort, con una decoración basada en materiales auténticos y artesanía autóctona.

Un resort di lusso in mezzo alla foresta tropicale vergine? L'architetto Kerry Hill ha risolto egregiamente questo compito. Perfino dalla spiaggia di sabbia finissima è quasi impossibile scorgere le 40 ville, 54 camere, nove suite, tre ristoranti, il centro fitness, la spa e la piscina. Essi sono stati realizzati nel maggior rispetto possibile per la natura selvaggia dell'isola Langkawi e dotati di tutti i comfort: l'arredamento si compone principalmente di materiali naturali e di artigianato locale.

The views of the rooms inside are fabulous, just like the outdoor views towards the turquoise color of Andaman Sea.

Die Einblicke in die Räume sind ebenso großartig, wie die Ausblicke auf die türkisfarbene Andamanische See.

A l'intérieur les pièces sont magnifiques, à l'extérieur le panorama sur la mer turquoise d'Andaman l'est tout autant.

Todas las vistas son cautivadoras, ya sea hacia las estancias como a los tonos turquesa del Mar de Adamán.

Gli interni sono di gusto eccezionale, così come la vista del mare turchino di Andaman.

The spaciousness *of the entrance hall is continued in the villas, whose living rooms and bedrooms almost indistinguishably merge with a generous bathroom. The Datai Bay Golf Course is only minutes away and framed by the rain forest and the Machinchang mountain range.*

Die Weitläufigkeit *der Empfangshalle setzt sich in den Villen fort, deren Wohn- und Schlafräume fast übergangslos in einen großzügigen Baderaum münden. Eingerahmt von Regenwald und der Machinchang-Bergkette liegt der Datai Bay Golf Course nur Minuten entfernt.*

Le hall *d'entrée est très spacieux, tout comme les villas, dont les pièces et les chambres se prolongent presque sans transition par une immense salle de bain. Niché entre la jungle et les Monts Machinchang, le Datai Bay Golf Course n'est qu'à quelques minutes.*

La espaciosidad *del hall no lo es menos en las habitaciones: sala de estar y dormitorio se prolongan sin cesuras hacia el baño. El Datai Bay Golf Course, ubicado a pocos minutos de distancia, está enmarcado por la selva y la montaña de Machinchang.*

La vastità *della hall non toglie nulla a quella delle ville, le cui sale e camere da letto sfociano quasi direttamente in uno spazioso bagno. Il percorso golfistico Datai Bay si trova a pochi minuti di distanza, nella cornice dalla foresta tropicale e del Monte Machinchang.*

The Datai Langkawi, Malaysia   191

The Sentosa Resort & Spa

Singapore, Singapore

The Sentosa Resort is only a few minutes away from the city center and not only attracts guests from around the world, but also Singapore's rich and famous. The reason is the restaurant "The Cliff"—a plan of the young Japanese designer Yasuhiro Koichi. As the name suggests, the restaurant is built on a cliff-head and from here guests can look down on the South China Sea. The finest seafood is served. Another attraction is the famous "Spa Botanica" with a comprehensive fitness program and, of course, around 27 acres of tropical gardens, which lead directly onto fabulous sandy beaches.

Nur wenige Minuten vom Stadtzentrum entfernt, lockt das Sentosa Resort nicht nur Gäste aus aller Welt, sondern auch Singapurs Prominenz an. Grund ist das Restaurant „The Cliff" – ein Entwurf des japanischen Designers Yasuhiro Koichi – das, wie der Name verrät, auf einen Felsvorsprung gebaut ist und von dem aus die Gäste auf das Südchinesische Meer blicken. Serviert wird feinstes Seafood. Ein weiterer Anziehungspunkt ist das renommierte „Spa Botanica" mit einem umfassenden Wellnessangebot und natürlich die rund elf Hektar große tropische Gartenanlage, die an herrliche Sandstrände anschließt.

A seulement quelques minutes du centre ville, le Sentosa Resort n'attire pas que les voyageurs du monde entier mais aussi les personnalités singapouriennes. Ils viennent surtout pour le restaurant « The Cliff » – un projet de l'architecte japonais Yasuhiro Koichi – qui, comme son nom l'indique, est bâti sur une falaise surplombant la mer de Chine du sud. On y sert de succulents fruits de mer. L'autre pôle d'attraction est le « Spa Botanica » avec sa palette complète de soins de remise en forme et naturellement les jardins tropicaux s'étendant sur onze hectares et bordant de magnifiques plages de sable.

A escasos minutos del centro de la ciudad se levanta el Sentosa Resort, centro de atracción no sólo para huéspedes famosos e internacionales sino también del país. Uno de los motivos para ello es el restaurante "The Cliff", concebido por el diseñador japonés Yasuhiro Koichi, que, como su nombre indica, se levanta sobre un acantilado y lanza la vista al Mar de la China Meridional. La carta propone mariscos de lo más selecto. Otros de los atractivos del lugar son el renombrado "Spa Botanica" con su amplia oferta de tratamientos Wellness, y el jardín tropical de once hectáreas que limita con unas playas magníficas.

A pochi minuti dal centro città, il Sentosa Resort attira non solamente ospiti da tutto il mondo, ma anche il jet set di Singapore. Motivo ne è il ristorante "The Cliff" – progettato dal designer giapponese Yasuhiro Koichi – costruito, come si intuisce dal nome, su di uno scoglio a picco sul mare, affacciato sul Mare Cinese Meridionale. La prelibata cucina è a base di pesce. Un'altra attrazione è la rinomata "Spa Botanica", con una ricca offerta di wellness e naturalmente il giardino tropicale grande circa undici ettari, che si estende fino alle splendide spiagge sabbiose.

Both 18-hole golf courses at the Sentosa Golf Club are not only beautiful, but above all they are challenging.

Die beiden 18-Loch-Plätze des Sentosa Golf Clubs sind nicht nur schön, sondern vor allem herausfordernd.

Les deux parcours 18-trous du Sentosa Golf Club sont beaux, mais surtout exigeants.

Belleza y reto se enfrentan en el campo de 18 hoyos del Sentosa Golf Club.

I due campi a 18 buche del Club golfistico Sentosa non sono soltanto belli, ma invitano anche alla sfida.

To compliment the 214 rooms and suites as well as four villas, the hotel offers a conference center and the Spa Botanica, which quickly advanced to one of the top addresses in Singapore.

Ergänzend zu den 214 Zimmern und Suiten sowie den vier Villen bietet das Hotel ein Konferenzcenter und das Spa Botanica, das schnell zu einer der ersten Adressen in Singapur avancierte.

Outre les 214 chambres et suites et les quatre villas, l'hôtel propose un centre de conférences et le Spa Botanica qui est vite devenu l'une des premières adresses de Singapour.

Además de las 214 habitaciones, cuatro villas y suites, el hotel dispone de un centro de conferencias y del Spa Botanica, lo que le ha convertido en una de las direcciones de élite de Singapur.

Oltre alle 214 camere e suite e alle quattro ville, l'hotel offre un centro congressi e la Spa Botanica, divenuta ben presto una delle mete più esclusive di Singapore.

Banyan Tree Phuket

Phuket, Thailand

In old legends, the Banyan tree is seen as a symbol of cheerfulness, wisdom, long life and tenacity. The resort, which is named after the tree, has adopted these principles. The 115 villas are like a fairytale. They are exotic and luxurious, each having a garden and open-air bathtub, with many of them even boasting their own swimming pool. The interior décor stimulates the senses and is relaxing at the same time. There are culinary treats from around the globe in the six restaurants. In the Saffron, the finest Thai cuisine is served. The 18 holes of Laguna Phuket Golf Club make a delightful scene, with a lake gracing nearly every fairway.

In alten Legenden gilt der Banyan-Baum als Symbol der Heiterkeit, Weisheit, Langlebigkeit und Spannkraft. Diese Grundlagen machte sich das gleichnamige Resort zu Eigen. Die 115 Villen sind wie aus einem Märchen. Exotisch und üppig, jede mit Garten und Freiluft-Badewanne, viele davon haben sogar ihr eigenes Schwimmbad. Die Einrichtung regt die Sinne an und schenkt gleichzeitig Entspannung. In den sechs Restaurants gibt es Kulinarisches rund um den Globus, im Saffron wird beste Thai-Küche serviert. Die 18 Löcher des Laguna Phuket Golf Clubs sind eine echte Augenweide. Fast jedes Fairway wird von einem See begleitet.

Dans les anciennes légendes le banyan est un arbre décrit comme un symbole de sérénité, sagesse, longévité et énergie. C'est sur ces bases que s'est développé ce resort. Les 115 villas semblent sortir d'un conte. Exotiques et luxuriantes, toutes possèdent leur jardin privé et une baignoire encastrée en plein air. Certaines ont même leur propre piscine. L'entourage éveille les sens tout en favorisant la relaxation. Les six restaurants servent des spécialités du monde entier et le Saffron propose une délicieuse cuisine thaï. Les 18 trous du Laguna Phuket Golf Club sont un plaisir pour la vue. Presque tous les fairways s'accompagnent d'un lac.

Según las antiguas leyendas el árbol Banyan es símbolo del gozo, la sabiduría, la longevidad y la energía. A partir de estas bases el resort ha hecho su razón de ser. Las 115 villas son de ensueño; todas ellas exóticas, exuberantes, y con jardín y bañera a cielo abierto; algunas incluso con piscina propia. La decoración de los interiores despierta los sentidos y transmite paz. Los seis restaurantes constituyen un verdadero centro culinario internacional. Saffron propone la cocina tailandesa más exquisita. El club de golf Laguna Phuket con sus 18 hoyos es un verdadero deleite. Casi todos sus Fairway están acompañados de un lago.

Nelle antiche leggende il Banyan Tree "baniano" è l'albero simbolo della serenità, della saggezza, della longevità e del vigore. Queste proprietà sono anche quelle dell'omonimo resort. Le 115 ville sono fiabesche: esotiche e lussureggianti, ognuna con giardino e vasca da bagno all'aperto, molte dotate addirittura di piscina privata. L'arredamento stimola i sensi e li distende al tempo stesso. I sei ristoranti offrono specialità culinarie da tutto il mondo, al Saffron si serve la migliore cucina thailandese. Le 18 buche del Laguna Phuket Golf Club sono una gioia per gli occhi: quasi ogni fairway è contornata da un ostacolo d'acqua.

In the consecrated garden of "The Sanctuary for the Senses", rose-petal baths and aromatic body packs are prepared. The hotel group's training center for spa employees is located here.

Im verwunschenen Garten des „The Sanctuary for the Senses" werden Rosenbäder und duftende Körperpackungen zubereitet. Hier befindet sich auch die Ausbildungsstätte der Hotelgruppe für Spa-Mitarbeiter.

Dans le jardin enchanté du « Sanctuaire des Sens », des bains à l'essence de rose et des soins enveloppants parfumés sont préparés. Il abrite également le centre de formation du groupe hôtelier pour le personnel du spa.

En el encantador jardín de "The Sanctuary for the Senses" se preparan baños de rosas y terapias corporales aromáticas. Aquí también está ubicado el centro de formación del hotel para los empleados del Spa.

Nel giardino fatato del "The Sanctuary for the Senses" si preparano bagni di rose ed impacchi profumati. Qui si trova anche il centro di formazione del gruppo alberghiero per i dipendenti della spa.

The Spa Pool Villa counts among as the most beautiful spa that the Asian world of wellness has to offer. Across the terrace and one's private pool, the view is of the lagoon and the ocean behind it.

Die Spa Pool Villa zählt zum Schönsten, was die asiatische Wellnesswelt zu bieten hat. Über die Terrasse und den eigenen Pool blickt man auf die Lagune und den dahinter liegenden Ozean.

La Spa Pool Villa est l'une des plus belles parmi les centres de bien-être existants en Asie. Au-delà de la terrasse et de sa propre piscine l'hôte peut admirer le lagon et l'océan au loin.

La Spa Pool Villa es una de las más bellas que existen en el mundo del Wellness asiático. Desde la terraza y la piscina propia, la vista abarca la laguna y el océano.

La villa Spa con piscina è tra le più belle del wellness asiatico. Dalla terrazza e dalla propria piscina lo sguardo si perde sulla laguna e sull'oceano alle sue spalle.

Banyan Tree Phuket *Phuket, Thailand* 199

Bo Phut Resort & Spa

Koh Samui, Thailand

Anyone who'd like to travel not only to faraway countries but also within himself has come to exactly the right spot at the Santiburi group's new boutique resort hotel. As soon as you have entered the lobby by a walkway flanked by pillars, you disappear into another world. Only 61 guest rooms are distributed in villas and the main house, all of them have a patio or balcony and are surrounded by a tropical garden. Fitness plays a central role here. Guests, who like more activity can visit the fitness center, go diving on the fabulous beach at Bo Phut or play golf on the Santiburi Samui Country Club's wonderful course.

Wer nicht nur in ferne Länder, sondern auch zu sich selbst reisen möchte, der ist im neuen Boutique-Resort-Hotel der Santiburi Gruppe genau richtig. Sobald man die Lobby über einen von Säulen flankierten Steg betreten hat, entschwindet man in eine andere Welt. Nur 61 Gästezimmer verteilen sich auf Villen und Haupthaus, alle mit Patio oder Balkon, umgeben von einem tropischen Garten. Wellness wird hier groß geschrieben. Wer es aktiver mag, besucht das Fitnesscenter, geht zum Tauchen am herrlichen Strand von Bo Phut oder spielt Golf auf dem wunderschönen Kurs vom Santiburi Samui Country Club.

Celui qui ne part pas seulement pour découvrir des pays lointains mais aussi pour se trouver, a atteint son but dans le nouveau Boutique Resort-Hotel de la chaîne hôtelière Santiburi. Dès qu'on pénètre dans le lobby par la passerelle flanquée de colonnes, on est transporté dans un autre monde. Villas et bâtiment principal abritent 61 chambres seulement, toutes avec patio ou balcon, entourées de jardins tropicaux. Ici, le bien-être est le maître mot. Les actifs visitent le centre de fitness, font de la plongée au large de la magnifique plage de Bo Phut ou jouent au golf sur le merveilleux terrain du Santiburi Samui Country Club.

Para quienes deseen vivir un viaje interior dentro de un viaje a países lejanos el nuevo Boutique Resort Hotel del grupo Santiburi es sin duda el lugar ideal. Ya la sensación que provoca entrar en el hall atravesando una pasarela flanqueada por columnas traslada a otro mundo. El resort dispone tan sólo de 61 habitaciones distribuidas entre villas y el edificio principal, todas ellas con patio o balcón, y rodeadas de un jardín tropical. Aquí Wellness está escrito en mayúsculas. Ahora bien, si se prefiere la actividad se puede visitar el gimnasio, hacer submarinismo en la fabulosa playa de Bo Phut o practicar golf en el fantástico recorrido del Santiburi Samui Country Club.

Chi desidera intraprendere un viaggio non solo in paesi lontani, ma anche in se stesso, non sbaglierà scegliendo il nuovo hotel boutique resort del gruppo Santiburi. Non appena si fa ingresso nella lobby da una passerella fiancheggiata da colonne, ci si trova in un altro mondo. Solo 61 camere sono distribuite nelle ville e nell'edificio principale, tutte con patio o balcone, circondate da un giardino tropicale. Qui tutto è all'insegna del wellness. Chi ama la vita più attiva, può frequentare il centro fitness, fare immersione sulla splendida spiaggia di Bo Phut oppure giocare a golf sul magnifico percorso del Santiburi Samui Country Club.

Hidden villas between palms and a sandy beach. Here, picture postcard views are a reality.

Versteckte Villen zwischen Palmen und Sandstrand. Hier wird Postkartenidylle zur Wirklichkeit.

Des villas cachées entre cocotiers et plage de sable. Les paysages idylliques de carte postale deviennent réalité ici.

Villas recogidas entre palmeras y playas de arena que hacen realidad la imagen idílica de postal.

Ville nascoste tra palme e spiaggia sabbiosa: qui l'idillio da cartolina diventa realtà.

The pool *offers a sea view. It's only a few steps from the rooms with four-poster beds to the white palm beach.*

Der Pool *bietet Meerblick. Von den Zimmern mit Himmelbetten zum weißen Palmen-Strand sind es nur ein paar Schritte.*

La piscine *a vue sur la mer. Quelques pas seulement séparent les chambres avec lit à baldaquin de la plage bordée de cocotiers.*

La piscina *tiene vistas al mar. Desde el dormitorio con cama con dosel a la playa blanca cuajada de palmeras hay sólo dos pasos.*

La piscina *ha vista sul mare. Soltanto pochi passi dividono le camere con il letto a cielo dalla spiaggia bianca circondata da palmeti.*

Bo Phut Resort & Spa *Koh Samui, Thailand*   203

Santiburi Resort

Koh Samui, Thailand

As well as Phuket, Koh Samui is one of the country's most popular holiday islands. The most luxurious resort there is also a place of relaxation, which in its perfect form invites you to do nothing. Twelve suites and 59 villas in the country's typical style, decorated with furniture from Siam, are hidden in a tropical garden that's right on the powdery fine sand and dream Mae Nam Beach. Couples especially enjoy a private jacuzzi on the terrace and like the "double treatments" offered in the spa after an active day's golf, tennis or sailing trip.

Neben Phuket ist Koh Samui eine der beliebtesten Ferieninseln des Landes. Das luxuriöseste Resort ist dort gleichsam ein Ort der Entspannung, der in seiner vollendeten Form zum Nichtstun einlädt. Zwölf Suiten und 59 Villen im landestypischen Stil, ausgestattet mit Möbeln aus Siam, verstecken sich in einem Tropengarten direkt am pulverfeinen Traumstrand Mae Nam. Vor allem Paare genießen den eigenen Whirlpool auf der Terrasse und freuen sich über die im Spa angebotenen „double treatments" nach einem aktiven Tag bei Golf, Tennis oder Segeltörn.

Avec Phuket, l'île de Koh Samui est l'une des destinations vacances les plus populaires. Ce resort d'un luxe extrême est un lieu de détente qui, de par sa perfection, invite à l'oisiveté. Douze suites et 59 villas de style traditionnel, aménagées avec des meubles originaires du Siam se dissimulent dans un jardin tropical directement au bord de la merveilleuse plage de sable fin de Mae Nam. Les couples d'amoureux jouissent de leur jacuzzi privé sur la terrasse et goûtent le plaisir des « doubles traitements » dispensés dans le spa après une journée d'activité au golf, au tennis ou à la voile.

Junto a Phuket la isla de Koh Samui es uno de los destinos de vacaciones preferidos del país. El lujoso resort es el súmmum de la relajación y el reposo. Las doce suites y 59 villas decoradas con muebles típicos de Siam se esconden en un jardín tropical a los pies de la playa de arena fina, Mae Nam. Las Parejas pueden disfrutar de Jacuzzi en la terraza y de las ofertas "double treatments" del Spa, así como de un día de golf, tenis o vela.

Accanto a Phuket, Koh Samui è una delle isole più ambite del paese come meta per le vacanze. Il resort più lussuoso è nel contempo un luogo di relax che, nella sua essenza più perfetta, invita al dolce far niente. Dodici suite e 59 ville in stile tipico del Paese, arredate con mobili siamesi, sono nascoste in un giardino tropicale che dà direttamente sulla favolosa spiaggia di sabbia finissima di Mae Nam. Dopo una giornata di attività giocando a golf o a tennis, o veleggiando in barca, soprattutto le coppie apprezzeranno la propria jacuzzi personale sulla terrazza e i "doppi trattamenti" offerti nella spa.

Anyone who's mastered the challenging golf course at the Santiburi Samui Country Club can look forward to a massage to loosen up those golfers' muscles.

Wer den anspruchsvollen Platz vom Santiburi Samui Country Club gemeistert hat, darf sich auf eine Massage zur Lockerung der Golfer-Muskeln freuen.

Après avoir relevé le défi du parcours très exigeant du Santiburi Samui Country Club, le golfeur savoure un massage pour l'assouplissement des muscles.

Una vez superado el reto del Santiburi Samui Country Club la recompensa es un masaje relajante del que gozarán los músculos del golfista.

Chi ha giocato sul difficile campo del Country Club Santiburi Samui, può concedersi il lusso di un massaggio per sciogliere i muscoli affaticati dal golf.

The view from the terrace of the clubhouse sweeps over the green on this estate, as far as the gulf of Thailand. The design of the rooms is simple and light and in contrast to the tropical surroundings.

Der Blick von der Clubhaus-Terrasse schweift über das Grün der Anlage bis zum Golf von Thailand. Schlicht und hell gestaltet, stehen die Räume im Kontrast zur tropischen Umgebung.

De la terrasse du Club House le regard se promène sur le vert du terrain jusqu'au Golfe de Thaïlande. Les pièces, simples et claires, contrastent avec l'exubérance tropicale.

El panorama desde la terraza del club abarca desde el verdor del complejo hasta el Golfo de Tailandia. Las habitaciones contrastan en austeridad y claridad con un denso entorno tropical.

La vista dalla terrazza del clubhouse si stende sul verde dell'area fino al golfo di Thailandia. Le sale sono sobrie e luminose, in contrasto con l'ambiente tropicale.

Santiburi Resort *Koh Samui, Thailand*

Kauri Cliffs Lodge

Matauri Bay, New Zealand

If you've seen the film "Lord of the Rings", you'll know all about New Zealand's dream landscape with its mystical forests, mountains and waterfalls. The Kauri Cliffs Lodge has exactly the same scenery and is situated above the "Bay of Islands". This is a hideaway for romantics and outdoor fans, who can explore the area along the 90 miles of beach by helicopter, jeep, on foot, by boat or on diving trips. The lodge is a relaxing place to retreat with 22 comfortable suites being distributed in eleven cottages, plus a restaurant, swimming pool, fitness center, spa, tennis and golf course and the only pink sandy beach in New Zealand.

Wer den Film „Herr der Ringe" gesehen hat, kennt die traumhafte Landschaft Neuseelands mit seinen mystischen Wäldern, Bergen und Wasserfällen. Genau die gleiche Kulisse findet sich bei der Kauri Cliffs Lodge, die oberhalb der „Bay of Islands" liegt. Ein Refugium für Romantiker und Outdoor-Fans, die die Gegend entlang des 145-Kilometer-Strandes per Helikopter, per Jeep, zu Fuß, per Boot oder bei Tauchgängen erkunden. Erholsamer Rückzugsort ist die Lodge, mit 22 komfortablen Suiten, verteilt in elf Cottages, plus Restaurant, Swimmingpool, Fitnesscenter, Spa, Tennis und Golfplatz und dem einzigen rosafarbenen Sandstrand von Neuseeland.

Quiconque a vu le film « Le Seigneur des Anneaux » connaît les paysages de rêve néo-zélandais avec ses forêts, montagnes et cascades mystiques. C'est sur cette toile de fond qu'est installé le Kauri Cliffs Lodge au-dessus de la « Bay of Islands ». Un refuge pour les romatiques et les fans d'activités de plein air qui explorent la région le long des 145 kilomètres de plage en hélicoptère, en jeep, à pied, en bateau ou en plongée. Le lodge est un endroit reposant, avec 22 suites confortables réparties sur onze cottages et comprenant restaurant, piscine, centre de fitness, spa, court de tennis et terrain de golf et où se trouve la seule plage de sable rose de Nouvelle-Zélande.

Quien haya visto "El señor de los anillos" ya conoce el cautivador paisaje neozelandés de bosques místicos, cumbres y cascadas. Un escenario puesto a disposición del Kauri Cliffs Lodge, ubicado en la parte alta del "Bay of Islands". El lugar es un auténtico hallazgo para románticos y amantes del aire libre, que tienen a su disposición 145 kilómetros de playa franqueables en helicóptero, Jeep, a pie, en barco o bien haciendo submarinismo. El descanso lo propone el Lodge con 22 confortables suites, repartidas entre once Cottages, restaurante, piscina, gimnasio, Spa, tenis y campo de golf, sin olvidar la única playa de arena rosa de toda Nueva Zelanda.

Chi ha visto il film "Il signore degli anelli" conosce il fantastico paesaggio della Nuova Zelanda con i suoi boschi mistici, montagne e cascate. Lo stesso scenario si trova al Kauri Cliffs Lodge, che sovrasta la "Bay of Islands". Un hideaway per i romantici e per gli amanti dell'outdoor, che possono esplorare la zona lungo la spiaggia di 145 chilometri in elicottero, in jeep, a piedi, in barca o facendo immersioni. Un ritrovo riposante è la lodge, con 22 confortevoli suite distribuite in undici cottage, a cui si aggiungono il ristorante, la piscina, il centro fitness, la spa, il campo da tennis e da golf e l'unica spiaggia rosa della Nuova Zelanda.

The Lodge is reminiscent of a plantation owner's manor house and is striking for its open, airy building style with light, cream colors in all the rooms.

Die an das Herrschaftshaus einer Plantage erinnernde Lodge besticht durch ihre offene, luftige Bauweise mit hellen Cremefarben in allen Räumen.

Le lodge qui ressemble à une maison de maître de plantation frappe par sa construction légère et aérée soulignée par l'utilisation de tons crème dans toutes les pièces.

El estilo de construcción abierto y libre y los tonos crema de las estancias recuerdan a la casa señorial de una plantación.

La lodge, che ricorda la tenuta di una piantagione, spicca per l'architettura aperta e ariosa, di color crema chiaro in tutte le sale.

The Lodge and pool offer spectacular panoramic views of the Pacific and the golf course.
Lodge und Pool bieten spektakuläre Panoramablicke auf den Pazifik und den Golfplatz.
Le lodge et la piscine offrent un panorama spectaculaire sur le Pacifique et le golf.
El Lodge y la piscina conceden unas vistas panorámicas espectaculares al Pacífico y al campo de golf.
La lodge e la piscina offrono scorci spettacolari sul Pacifico e sul campo da golf.

210   Kauri Cliffs Lodge   *Matauri Bay, New Zealand*

Kauri Cliffs Lodge *Matauri Bay, New Zealand* 211

Selected Courses

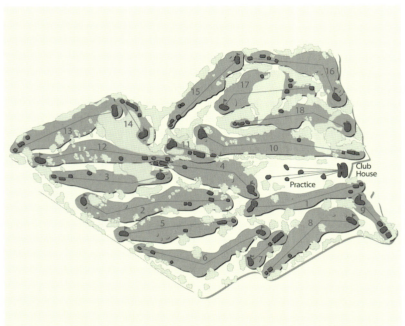

Belle Mare Plage The Resort, Mauritius

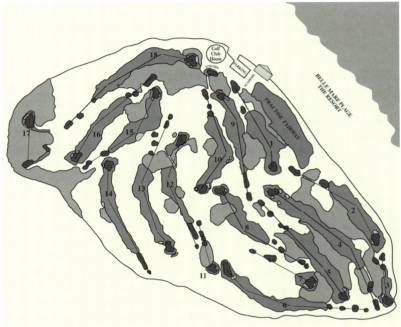

Belle Mare Plage The Resort, Mauritius

Stoke Park Club, England

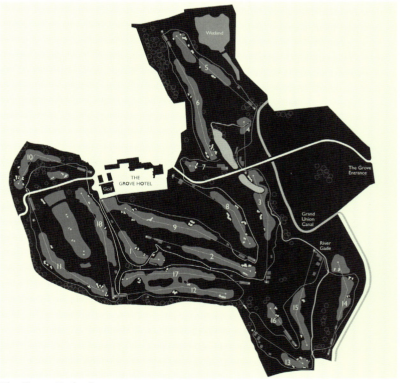

The Grove, England

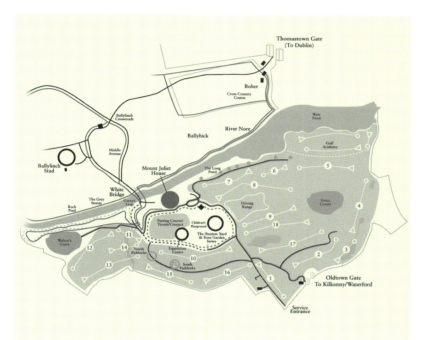

Mount Juliet Conrad, Ireland

Adare Manor Hotel & Golf Resort, Ireland

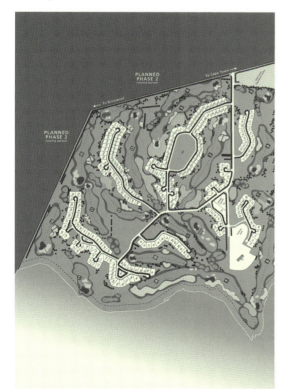

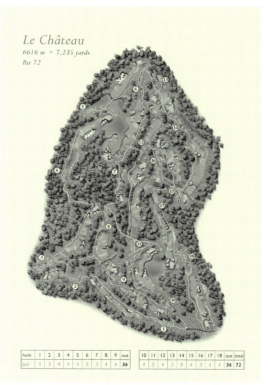

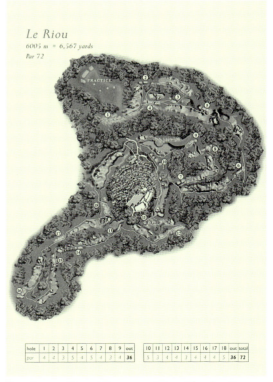

The Western Cape Hotel & Spa, South Africa

Four Seasons Resort Provence at Terre Blanche, France

Four Seasons Resort Provence at Terre Blanche, France

Selected Courses   213

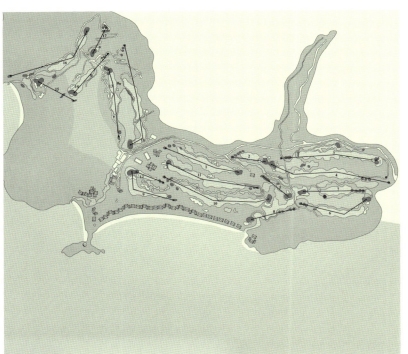

Lénuria Resort of Praslin, Seychelles

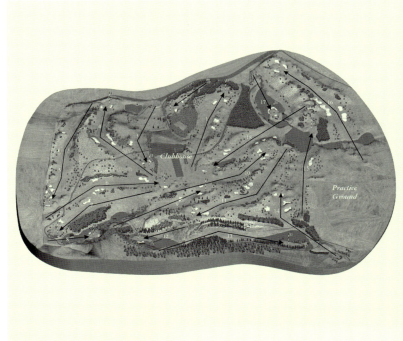

Marriott Druids Glen Hotel & Country Club, Ireland

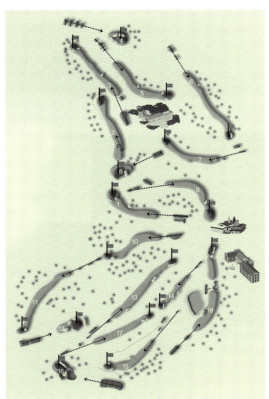

ArabellaSheraton Golf Hotel Son Vida, Spain

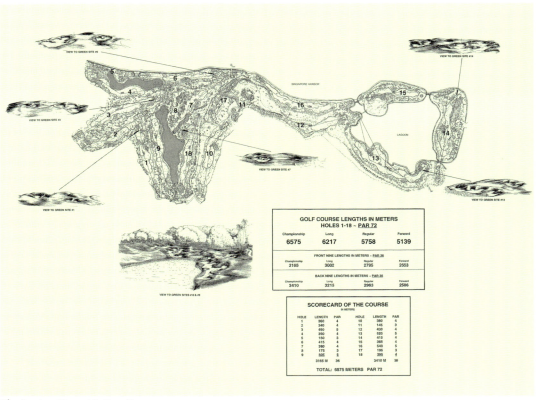

The Sentosa Resort & Spa, Singapore

One&Only Ocean Club, Bahamas

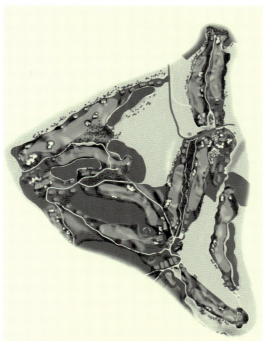

One&Only Ocean Club, Bahamas

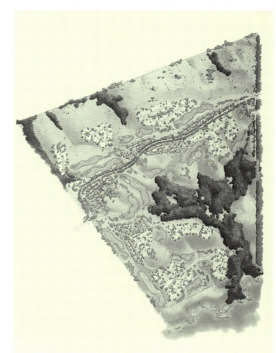

One&Only Ocean Club, Bahamas

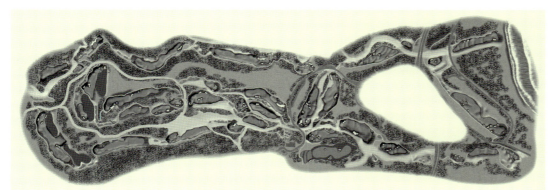

One&Only Palmilla, Mexico

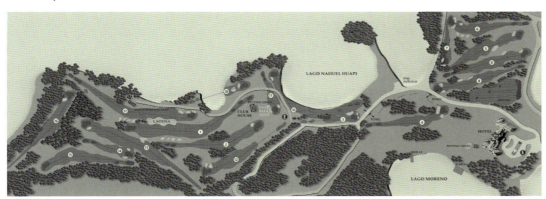

Llao Llao Resort, Argentina

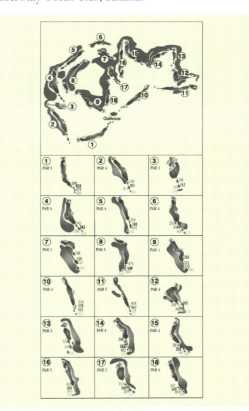

Four Seasons Resort Carmelo, Uruguay

Selected Courses 215

Index

Hawaii

Maui

Four Seasons Resort Maui at Wailea
3900 Wailea Alanui, Wailea, Maui, Hawaii 96753, USA
T +1 (808) 874 8000, F +1 (808) 874 2244
www.fourseasons.com
377 rooms including 75 suites. 3 restaurants. Spa, 13 treatment rooms plus 3 oceanside Hawaiian massage "hales". Water sports, scuba center, tennis courts. 5 golf courses within 10 minutes. 35 minutes from Kahului Airport.

Wailea Golf & Country Club, 100 Waileas, Golf Club Drive,
Wailea, Maui, Hawai 96753-4000, USA
T +1 (808) 875 7450, F +1 (808) 875 5114
www.waileagolf.com, email: reservations@waileagolf.com
Emerald Course: 18 holes, 6825 yards, par 72, design: Robert Trent Jones Jr.
Gold Course: 18 holes, 7078 yards, par 72, design: Robert Trent Jones Jr.
Blue Course: 18 holes, 6758 yards, par 72, design: Arthur Jack Snyder

California

Dana Point

St. Regis Resort, Monarch Beach
One Monarch Beach Resort, Dana Point, California 92629, USA
T +1 (949) 234 3200, F +1 (949) 234 3201
www.stregismonarchbeach.com
400 rooms including 74 suites and 2 Presidential Suites. 6 ocean-view restaurants. 3 pools, spa. Meeting facilities. 60 minutes from both Los Angeles and San Diego Airport.

Monarch Beach Golflinks
22 Monarch Beach Resort, Dana Point, California 92629, USA
T +1 (949) 240 8247, F +1 (949) 234 3201
18 holes, 6340 yards, par 70, design: Robert Trent Jones Jr.

Arizona

Scottsdale

Four Seasons Resort Scottsdale at Troon North
10600 East Crescent Moon Drive, Scottsdale, Arizona 85262-8342, USA
T +1 (480) 515 5700, F +1 (480) 515 5599
www.fourseasons.com
210 guest rooms and suites. 3 restaurants, lobby lounge. Spa, health club, beauty salon. Pool and childrens pool. 2 tennis courts. Priority use of the Troon North championship golf courses. 45 minutes from Phoenix Sky Harbor International Airport.

Troon North Golf Club, 10320 E Dynamite Blvd, Scottsdale, Arizona 85262, USA
T +1 (480) 585 5300, F +1 (480) 585 5161
www.troonnorthgolf.com, email: mhenritze@troongolf.com
Pinnacle Course: 18 holes, 7044 yards, par 72, design: Tom Weiskopf
Monument Course: 18 holes, 7028 yards, par 72, design: Tom Weiskopf/Jay Morrish

Bahamas

Paradise Island

One&Only Ocean Club
Paradise Island, Bahamas
T +1 (242) 363 2501, F +1 (242) 363 2424
www.oneandonlyresorts.com
106 rooms including 14 suites nestled in different buildings, garden cottages and villas. 2 restaurants, pool terrace café, gourmet in-room dining. Spa, 2 pools. 6 tennis-courts, complimentary non-motorized watersports. A short ride from Nassau International Airport.

One&Only Ocean Club Paradise Island, Bahamas
T +1 (242) 363 6682, F +1 (242) 363 2424
www.oneandonlyresorts.com
18 holes, 7065 yards, par 72, design: Tom Weiskopf

Mexico

Costalegre

El Tamarindo
Km 7,5 Carretera Melaque to Puerto Vallarta, Cihuatlán, Costa Careyes, 48970 Jalisco, Mexico
T. +52 (315) 351 5032, F +52 (315) 351 5070
www.mexicoboutiquehotels.com
28 villas with private plunge pool. Restaurant, bar, lounge. 3 private beaches and private pier. Pool, jungle spa. Tennis courts. 3,5 hours south of Puerto Vallarta and 50 minutes north of Manzanillo Airport.

El Tamarindo, Km 7,5 Carretera Melaque to Puerto Vallarta, Cihuatlán, Costa Careyes, 48970 Jalisco, Mexico
T +52 (322) 221 2277, F +52 (322) 221 2255
www.mexicoboutiquehotels.com, email: thetamarindo@mexicoboutiquehotels.com
18 holes, 6750 yards, par 72, design: Robert Trent Jones Jr./David Fleming

Los Cabos

One&Only Palmilla
Km 7,5 Carretera Transpeninsular, 23400 San José Del Cabo, Mexico
T +52 (624) 146 7000, F +52 (624) 146 7001
www.oneandonlyresorts.com
152 rooms, 20 suites with patio or balcony and 2 villas. Personal butler service. 2 restaurants, outdoor bar and lounge. Spa, fitness center, watersports. Conference center, ballroom. 20 minutes from José del Cabo International Airport.

One&Only Palmilla Golf Club, Km 7,5 Carretera Transpeninsular, 23400 San José Del Cabo, Mexico
T +52 (624) 146 7000, F +52 (624) 146 7001
www.palmillaresort.com, email: reservations@oneandonlypalmilla.com
27 holes, 6900 yards, par 72 for 18 holes, design: Jack Nicklaus

Costa Rica

Peninsula Papagayo

Four Seasons Resort Costa Rica at Peninsula Papagayo
Peninsula Papagayo, Guanacaste, Costa Rica
T +11 (50) 6696 0000, F +11 (50) 6696 0500
www.fourseasons.com
165 rooms including 37 suites—some with private plunge pool. 3 restaurants. Pool, children's pool. Fitness center, spa, treatments. 40 minutes by air from San José International Airport.

Four Seasons Golf Club Costa Rica at Peninsula Papagayo, Peninsula Papagayo, Guanacaste, Costa Rica
T +11 (50) 6696 0000, F +11 (50) 6696 0500
www.fourseasons.com
18 holes, 6788 yards, par 72, design: Arnold Palmer

Argentina

San Carlos de Bariloche

Llao Llao Resort
Av. Ezequiel Bustillo, Km 25, R8409ALN Bariloche-Patagonia, Argentina
T +54 (2944) 448 530, F +54 (2944) 445 781
www.llaollao.com
147 rooms, 11 suites, 1 cabin. 2 restaurants, lobby bar, winter garden, club house. Spa and healthclub. Meeting facilities. Nestled between Lake Nahuel Huapi and Lake Moreno, 2 hours flight from Buenos Aires and 35 km from San Carlos de Bariloche Airport.

Llao Llao Resort, Av. Ezequiel Bustillo, Km 25, R8409ALN, Bariloche-Patagonia, Argentina
T +54 (2944) 448 530, F +54 (2944) 445 781
www.llaollao.com
18 holes, 5865 yards, par 70, design: Emilio Ferra

Uruguay

Carmelo

Four Seasons Resort Carmelo
Ruta 21, Km 262, Carmelo, Dpto. de Colonia, Uruguay
T +598 (542) 9000, F +598 (542) 9999
www.fourseasons.com
20 bungalows and 24 two-level duplex suites. 3 restaurants, 2 lounges. Spa, health club, sauna, massage. Tennis. 30 minutes by small plane from Buenos Aires International Airport.

Four Seasons Carmelo Golf Club, Ruta 21, Km 262, Carmelo, Dpto. de Colonia, Uruguay
T +598 (542) 9000, F +598 (542) 9999
www.fourseasons.com
18 holes, 7158 yards, par 72, design: Randy Thompson/Kelly Moran

Scotland

Perthshire

The Gleneagles Hotel
Auchterarder, Perthshire PH3 1NF, Scotland
T +44 (1764) 662 231, F +44 (1764) 662 134
www.gleneagles.com
269 rooms including 16 suites. 2 restaurants—1 of them Michelin starred, club house, club and bar. Spa. Tennis. Meeting facilities. 1 hours drive to Edinburgh and Glasgow airports.

The Gleneagles Hotel, Auchterarder, Perthshire, Scotland PH3 1NF
T +44 (1764) 662 231, F +44 (1764) 662 134
www.gleneagles.com, email: resort.sales@gleneagles.com
PGA Centenary Course: 18 holes, 7088 yards, design: Jack Nicklaus
The King's Course: 18 holes, 6790 yards, par 71, design: James Braid
The Queen's Course: 18 holes, 5965 yards, par 68, design: James Braid
Wee Course: 9 holes, 1418 yards, par 27, design: Georg Alexander/James Kidd

England

Buckinghamshire

Stoke Park Club
Park Road, Stoke Poges, Buckinghamshire SL2 4PG, Great Britain
T +44 (1753) 717 171, F +44 (1753) 717 181
www.stokeparkclub.com
21 rooms including 3 suites. 2 restaurants and a members lounge and bar. Spa. Ballroom and 8 conference rooms including 3 rooms fully licensed civil ceremonies. Established 1908 as the 1st country club in Britain. 7 miles from London Heathrow.

Stoke Park Club, Park Road, Stoke Poges, Bucks SL2 4PG, Great Britain
T +44 (1753) 717 171, F +44 (1753) 717 181
www.stokepark.co.uk, email: info@stokeparkclub.co.uk
27 holes, 9922 yards, 18 holes, par 74/73, design: Colt, Alison, Jackson

Hertfordshire

The Grove
The Grove, Chandler's Cross, Hertfordshire WD3 4TG, Great Britain
T +44 (1923) 807 807, F +44 (1923) 221 008
www.thegrove.co.uk
227 rooms and suites. 3 restaurants and lounge. Heated swimming pool, Spa. 2 tennis courts. Kid's club. Meeting facilities. 30 minutes drive from London Heathrow.

The Grove, Chandler's Cross, Hertfordshire WD3 4TG, Great Britain
T +44 (1923) 807 807, F +44 (1923) 221 008
www.thegrove.co.uk, email: info@thegrove.co.uk
18 holes, 7152 yards, par 72, design: Kyle Phillips

Ireland

County Wicklow

Marriott Druids Glen Hotel & Country Club
Newtownmountkennedy, County Wicklow, Ireland
T +353 (1) 287 0800, F +353 (1) 287 0801
www.marriott.ie/dubgs
137 rooms, 11 suites. 2 restaurants, bar. Meeting facilities. Spa and health club, 4 treatment rooms, 18 m indoor swimming pool, sauna. 40 km from Dublin International Airport.

Marriott Druids Glen Hotel, Newtownmountkennedy, County Wicklow, Ireland
T +353 (1) 287 0800, F +353 (1) 287 0801
www.Marriott.ie, email: mhrs.dubgs.reservations@marriottdruidsglen.com
Druids Glen Course: 18 holes, 7464 yards, par 71, design: P. Ruddy/T. Craddock
Druids Heath Course: 18 holes, 7434 yards, par 71, design: Pat Ruddy

Adare

Adare Manor Hotel & Golf Resort
Adare Manor Hotel & Golf Resort, Adare, County Limerick, Ireland
T +353 (61) 396 566, F +353 (61) 396 124
www.adaremanor.com
63 Manor House bedrooms, 11 Clubhouse bedrooms and 25 self catering Townhouses. Spa, World-class dining facilities. Equestrian center. Conference facilities for up to 250 people.

Adare Golfclub, Adare, County Limerick, Ireland
T +353 (61) 395 044, F +353 (61) 396 987
www.adaremanor.com, email: golf@adaremanor.com
18 holes, 7125 yards, par 72, design: Robert Trent Jones Sr.

County Clare

Dromoland Castle
Newmarket-on-Fergus, County Clare, Ireland
T +353 (61) 368 144, F +353 (61) 363 355
www.dromoland.ie
100 rooms including a Presidential Suite. 2 restaurants, afternoon tea in the Drawing Room. Spa. Tennis. Conference facilities for up to 480 people. 8 miles from Shannon Airport.

Dromoland Castle, Newmarket-on-Fergus, County Clare, Ireland
T +353 (61) 368 144, F +353 (61) 363 355
www.dromoland.ie, email: sales@dromoland.ie
18 holes, 6845 yards, par 72, design: Ron Kirby/J.B. Carr

County Kildare

The K Club Golf Resort
The K Club, Straffan, County Kildare, Ireland
T +353 (1) 601 7200, F +353 (1) 601 7299
www.kclub.ie
69 hotel rooms, including Superior, Deluxe, River Room and 12 suites. The Imperial Suite with 2 bedrooms, the Viceroy Suite with Jacuzzi. 25 Garden and Courtyard Suites. 2 restaurants, 3 bars. Spa. 10 miles from Dublin International Airport.

The K Club, Straffan, County Kildare, Ireland
T +353 (1) 601 7200, F +353 (1) 601 7299
www.kclub.ie, email: resortsales@kclub.ie
Palmer Course: 18 holes, 7337 yards, par 72, design: Arnold Palmer
Smurfit Course: 18 holes, 7277 yards, par 72, design: Arnold Palmer

County Kilkenny

Mount Juliet Conrad
Thomastown, County Kilkenny, Ireland
T +353 (56) 777 3000, F +353 (56) 777 3019
www.conradhotels.com
32 rooms in Mount Juliet House, 16 Club rooms at the Hunters Yard, 10 Rose Garden Lodges. Dining Room, restaurant, bar. Spa, sauna, swimming pool. 70 miles south of Dublin Airport, 10 miles southeast of Kilkenny.

Mount Juliet, Thomastown, County Killkenny, Ireland
T +353 (56) 777 3064, F +353 (56) 777 3078
www.mountjuliet.com, email: info@mountjuliet.ie
18 holes, 7300 yards, par 72, design: Jack Nicklaus

Germany

Donaueschingen

Der Öschberghof
Golfplatz 1, 78166 Donaueschingen, Germany
T +49 (771) 84 612, F +49 (771) 84 600
www.oeschberghof.com
73 rooms and suites. 2 restaurants, bar. Wellness facilities, indoor pool, beauty treatments. Conference facilities for up to 200 people. 125 km from Stuttgart Airport, 90 km from Zurich.

Der Öschberghof, Golfplatz 1, 78166 Donaueschingen, Germany
T +49 (771) 84 525, F +49 (771) 84 540
www.oeschberghof.de, email: info@oeschberghof.de
18 holes, 7051 yards, par 74, design: Deutsche Golf-Consult
9 holes, 2252 yards, par 31, design: Deutsche Golf-Consult

Friedrichsruhe

Schlosshotel Friedrichsruhe
Kärcherstraße, 74639 Friedrichsruhe/Zweiflingen, Germany
T +49 (7941) 608 70, F +49 (7941) 614 68
www.friedrichsruhe.de
The resort consists in main building, hunting lodge and garden-mansions. Gourmet restaurant. In- and outdoor pool, beauty farm, sauna. Tennis. Conference facilities for up to 120 people. 1 hour drive from Stuttgart Airport.

Golf-Club Heilbronn-Hohenlohe e.V., Hofgasse 12, 74639 Friedrichsruhe, Germany
T +49 (7941) 920 810, F +49 (7941) 920 819
www.friedrichsruhe.de, email: golf@friedrichsruhe.de
18 holes, 6399 yards, par 72, design: Donald Harradine

Italy

Lake Garda

Palazzo Arzaga Hotel Spa & Golf Resort
25080 Carzago di Calvagese della Riviera, Brescia, Italy
T +39 (030) 680 600, F +39 (030) 680 6270
www.palazzoarzaga.it
83 rooms and suites in 3 buildings: the 15th century mansion, "Residenza San Martino", "Residenza dei Castagni". Restaurant, enotheca, clubhouse. Spa. Conference facilities for up to 250 persons, receptions for up to 1000 persons on the terrace. Situated between the Alps and Lake Garda, 30 minutes from Verona.

Palazzo Arzaga Hotel, Spa & Golf Resort, 25080 Carzago di Calvagese della Riviera, Brescia, Italy
T +39 (030) 680 600, F +39 (030) 680 6270
www.palazzoarzaga.com, email: info@palazzoarzaga.com
Course I: 18 holes, 6795 yards, par 72, design: Jack Nicklaus II
Course II: 9 holes, 3310 yards, par 36, design: Gary Player/Jack Nicklaus II

France

Tourrettes

Four Seasons Resort Provence at Terre Blanche
Domaine de Terre Blanche, 83440 Tourrettes, Var, France
T +33 (4) 9439 9000, F +33 (4) 9439 9001
www.fourseasons.com
115 suites with private terraces. 4 restaurants. Pool and childrens pool. Spa Villa and Fitness Villa. Banquet facilities. 45 minutes from Nice International Airport.

Golf de Terre Blanche, 83440 Tourrettes, Frankreich
T +33 (4) 9439 9000, F +33 (4) 9439 9001
www.fourseasons.com
Le Château Course: 18 holes, 7235 yards, par 72, design: Dave Thomas
Le Riou Course: 18 holes, 6567 yards, par 72, design: Dave Thomas

Evian-les-Bains **Evian Royal Resort**
Rive Sud du Lac de Genève, 74501 Evian-les-Bains, France
T +33 (450) 268 500, F +33 (450) 756 100
www.evianroyalresort.com
153 rooms including 11 suites. Le Café Royal, lounge restaurant, rôtisserie, Spa Cuisine, pool bar, bar. Casino. Spa. 4 green tennis set courts, 1 indoor court and 1 synthetic grass court. Climbing wall. Conference facilities. Located at the south bank of Lake Geneva.

Evian Masters Golf Club, 74500 Evian, Haute Savoie, France
T +33 (450) 268 500, F +33 (450) 756 100
www.evianroyalresort.com, email: reservation@evianroyalresort.com
18 holes, 6568 yards, par 72, design: Cabell B. Robinson

Spain

Marbella **Rio Real Golf Hotel**
Urbanización Río Real, 29600 Marbella, Spain
T +34 (952) 765 732, F +34 (952) 772 140
www.rioreal.com
16 rooms, 14 suites. 2 restaurants, 2 bars. Outdoor swimming pool. Meeting facilities. 50 km from Málaga Airport.

Rio Real Golf Hotel, Urbanización Río Real, 29600 Marbella, Spain
T +34 (952) 765 732, F +34 (952) 772 140
www.rioreal.com, email: info@rioreal.com
18 holes, 6743 yards, par 72, design: Javier Arana

Marbella **Villa Padierna**
Ctra. N-340, Km 166, 29679 Marbella, Spain
T +34 (952) 889 150, F +34 (952) 889 160
www.hotelvillapadierna.com
112 rooms and suites, 4 restaurants and bar. Meeting and conference facilities. 75 from Málaga International Airport.

Flamingos Golf Club, Ctra. de Cádiz, Km 166, Salida: Cancelada, 29679 Marbella, Spain
T +34 (952) 889 150, F +34 (952) 889 160
www.flamingos-golf.com, email: info@flamingos-golf.com
Flamingos Course: 18 holes, 6452 yards, par 72, design: Antonio G. Garrido
Executive Course: 9 holes, par 27, design: Antonio G. Garrido

Estepona **Kempinski Hotel Bahía Estepona**
Carretera de Cádiz, Km 159, 29680 Estepona, Málaga, Spain
T +34 (952) 809 500, F +34 (952) 809 550
www.kempinski-spain.com
133 rooms and 15 suites with sea view and balcony or terrace. 3 restaurants and 2 bars. Beauty and wellness center. Surrounded by golf courses: more than 40 golf courses can be found between Málaga and Sotogrande, including the famous Valderrama Club. 18 km from Marbella.

Denia **Denia Marriott La Sella Golf Resort & Spa**
Alqueria Ferrando, Jesus Pobre, 03749 Denia, Alicante, Spain
T +34 (96) 645 4054, F +34 (96) 575 7880
www.marriott.com
178 rooms, 8 suites. 3 restaurants—1 of them at hole 19. Alanya Spa, fitness center. Kid's club. 7 meeting rooms. 100 km from both—Alicante and Valencia Airport.

Denia Marriott La Sella Golf Resort, Alqueria Ferrando, Jesus Pobre, 03749 Denia, Alicante, Spain
T +34 (96) 645 4054, F +34 (96) 575 7880
www.marriott.de
18 holes, 6072 yards, 72 par, design: Juan de la Cuadra

Murcia **Hyatt Regency La Manga**
Los Belones, 30385 Cartagena, Murcia, Spain
T +34 (968) 33 1234, F +34 (968) 33 1235
www.hyatt.com
189 rooms and suites with golf and poolview. More than 20 restaurants and bars. In- and outdoor swimming pools. Spa, wellness center. 28 tennis courts, squash. 120 km from Alicante airport.

Golf at La Manga Club, 30385 Los Belones, Cartagena, Murcia, Spain
T +34 (968) 175 000, F +34 (968) 175 058
www.golf.lamangaclub.com, email: golf@lamangaclub.com
South Course: 18 holes, 7107 yards, par 73, design: R. Putman/A. Palmer
North Course: 18 holes, 6291 yards, par 71, design: Robert Putman
West Course: 18 holes, 6529 yards, par 73, design: Dave Thomas

Cádiz **San Roque Club**
C.N. 340, Km 127, 11360 San Roque, Cádiz, Spain
T +34 (956) 613 030, F +34 (956) 613 012
www.sanroqueclub.com
100 rooms and suites. 2 restaurants, bar and terrace. Heated lagoon pool, private beach club. Tennis court, equestrian center. Meeting facilities for up to 70 people. 1½ hours drive from Málaga International Airport and 20 minutes from Gibraltar Airport.

The San Roque Club, C.N. 340, Km 127, 11360 San Roque, Cádiz, Spain
T +34 (956) 613 030, F +34 (956) 613 012
www.sanroqueclub.com, email: info@sanroqueclub.com
Old Course: 18 holes, 7101 yards, par 72, design: Dave Thomas
New Course: 18 holes, 7246 yards, par 72, design: Perry Dye

Majorca **ArabellaSheraton Golf Hotel Son Vida**
Carrer de la Vinagrella, 07013 Palma de Mallorca, Spain
T +34 (971) 787 100, F +34 (971) 787 200
www.arabellasheratonhotels.com
93 rooms, including 22 suites and one Grand Suite. 2 restaurants and lobby bar. Altira Spa. Outdoor pool. Meeting and conference facilities. 15 minutes from Palma and 20 minutes from the airport.

Golf Son Vida, Urbanización Son Vida, 07013 Palma de Mallorca, Spain
T +34 (971) 791 210
www.sonvidagolf.com, email: info@sonvidagolf.com
18 holes, 6125 yards, par 71, design: F.W. Hawtree

Golf Son Muntaner, Carretera de Son Vida, 07013 Palma de Mallorca, Spain
T +34 (971) 783 030, F +34 (971) 783 031
www.sonmuntanergolf.com, email: info@sonmuntanergolf.com
18 holes, 6941 yards, par 72, design: Kurt Rossknecht

Morocco

Marrakech **Amanjena**
Route de Ouarzazate, Km 12, 40000 Marrakech, Morocco
T +212 (4) 440 3353, F +212 (4) 440 3477
www.amanjena.com
32 pavilions with fireplace, private pool and garden. 6 Maisons. Al-Hamra Suite, 180 m² pavilion, two minzahs and its own 40 m² pool. 3 restaurants and bar. Library. Heated swimming pool. Wellness center with 2 hammams. 5 miles south of the center of Marrakech.

Golf d'Amelkis, Route de Ouarzazate, Marrakech, Morocco
T +212 (4) 440 4414, F +212 (4) 440 4415
18 holes, 7280 yards, par 72, design: Cabell B. Robinson

Egypt

Cairo **Oberoi Mena House**
Pyramids' Road, Giza, Cairo, Egypt
T +20 (2) 383 3222, F +20 (2) 383 7777
www.oberoihotels.com
523 rooms and suites nestled in the Palace and Garden wings. Cabana style rooms by the swimming pool. 4 restaurants, pool restaurant and Sultan Bar with panoramic views of the pyramids. Outdoor swimming pool in the garden. Tennis courts. Banquet facilities up to 520 people. 45 minutes drive from Cairo International Airport.

Mena House Golf Course, Pyramids' Road, Giza, Cairo, Egypt
T +20 (2) 383 3222, F +20 (2) 383 7777
www.oberoihotels.com, email: obmhogm@oberoi.com.eg
9 holes, 2674 yards, par 34, design: Roy Wilson

Mauritius

Poste de Flacq **Belle Mare Plage The Resort**
Poste de Flacq, Mauritius, Indian Ocean
T +230 (402) 2600, F +230 (402) 2616
www.bellemareplagehotel.com
235 rooms and suites. 7 restaurants, 2 of them on the beachside, 4 bars and beach bar. Spa and fitness center with Shiseido pavilion. Watersports. 40 km from the airport. 1 hour drive and 15 minutes flight by helicopter.

Belle Mare Plage The Resort, Poste de Flacq, Mauritius, Indian Ocean
T +230 (402) 2735, F +230 (415) 5228
www.bellemareplagehotel.com, email: resa@bellemareplagehotel.com
The Legend: 18 holes, 6581 yards, par 72, design: Hugh Baiocchi
The Links: 18 holes, 6498 yards, par 71, design: Rodney Wright/Peter Allis

Seychelles

Praslin **Lémuria Resort of Praslin**
Anse Kerlan, Praslin, Seychelles
T +248 281 281, F +248 281 001
www.lemuriaresort.com
96 suites, 8 villas, 1 Presidential Villa, all oriented towards the Indian Ocean. 2 restaurants, grill at the beach. 3 bars and beach bar. Health and beauty spa with Guerlain Institute. Water- and inland sports, tennis. Situated on the island of Praslin approximately 15 minutes by plane from the main island of Mahé. 10 minutes drive from Praslin airport.

Lémuria of Praslin, Anse Kerlan, Praslin, Seychelles
T +248 281 281, F +248 281 001
www.lemuriaresort.com, email: resa@lemuriaresort.com
18 holes, 6076 yards, par 70, design: Marc A. Farry/Rodney Wright

South Africa

Hermanus

The Western Cape Hotel & Spa
Hermanus, Western Cape, South Africa
T +27 (28) 284 0000, F +27 (28) 284 0011
www.arabellasheraton.co.za
145 rooms and suites including 2 Presidential Suites. 2 restaurants, Laguna Lounge, pool bar and cigar bar. Spa. Conference facilities. 60 minutes drive from Capetown International Airport.

Arabella Golf Club, P.O. Box 593, Kleinmond, 7195 Cape Province, South Africa
T +27 (28) 284 0000, F +27 (28) 284 0011
www.arabellasheraton.co.za, email: golf@wchs.co.za
18 holes, 6978 yards, par 72, design: Peter Matkovich

Kwa Zulu Natal

Zimbali Lodge
Zimbali Estate, Kwa Zulu Natal North Coast, South Africa
T +27 (32) 538 1007, F +27 (32) 538 1019
www.sunint.co.za
76 rooms and suites nestled in 8 individual lodges. Restaurant, lounge and pool bar. Health and beauty spa, swimming pool. Tennis courts. Meeting facilities. Located 25 km from Ballito, 45 km from Durban, 650 km from Johannesburg.

Zimbali Golf Course, P.O. Box 770, Jukskei Park, 2153 Gauteng, South Africa
T +27 (31) 762 2066, F +27 (32) 538 1019
www.zimbali.org, email: travel@zimbali.org
18 holes, 7134 yards, par 72, design: Tom Weiskopf

Knysna

Pezula Resort Hotel & Spa
Knysna, South Africa
T +27 (44) 302 3333, F +27 (44) 302 3303
www.pezula.com
78 suites including 2 Presidential Suites. Restaurant, wine cellar, Whiskey Bar and cigar lounge bar. Private dining. Spa and gym. Tennis, horse riding. Conference facilities. Pezula Aviation Service. 5 driving hours from Cape Town, 45 minutes from George Airport.

Pezula Championship Golf Course, Knysna, South Africa
T +27 (44) 302 5333, F +27 (44) 384 1277
www.pezula.com, email: golf@pezula.com
18 holes, 7005 yards, par 72, design: Ronald Fream

Indonesia

Bintan Island

Banyan Tree Bintan
Site A4, Lagoi, Bintan Island, Indonesia
T +62 (770) 693 100, F +62 (770) 693 200
www.banyantree.com
70 villas. Jacuzzi Villas with Jacuzzis on their sun decks, Pool Villas with own swimming pool. 3 restaurants, in-villa dining. Swimming pool. Windsurfing, other watersports nearby. 45 minutes by high-speed catamaran from Singapore, followed by a 10 minutes transfer.

Laguna Bintan Golf Club, Site A4, Lagoi, Bintan Island, Indonesia
T +62 (770) 693 188, F +62 (770) 693 288
www.banyantree.com, email: golf-bintan@banyantree.com
18 holes, 6889 yards, par 72, design: Greg Norman

Malaysia

Langkawi

The Andaman
Jalan Teluk Datai, 07000 Pulau Langkawi, Kedah Darul Aman, Malaysia
T +60 (4) 959 1088, F +60 (4) 959 1168
www.ghmhotels.com
186 air-conditioned rooms and suites. 3 restaurants, poolside terrace, beach bar and lobby lounge. Spa, fitness center. Billiards- and games room. Kid's club. Meeting facilities. 30 minutes from Langkawi International Airport.

Golf Club Datai Bay, Jalan Teluk Datai, 07000 Langkawi, Malaysia
T +60 (4) 959 2700, F +60 (4) 959 2216
www.dataigolf.com
18 holes, 6555 yards, par 72, design: Landmarks Berhad

Langkawi

The Datai
Jalan Teluk Datai, 07000 Pulau Langkawi, Kedah Darul Aman, Malaysia
T +60 (4) 959 2500, F +60 (4) 959 2600
www.ghmhotels.com
54 rooms, 9 suites, 40 villas including 5 pool villas with private plunge pools, The Datai Suite with 2 bedrooms, spacious living room and fully equipped kitchen. 3 restaurants, beach club, dining room, Thai Pavilion, lobby lounge bar. Spa. Set in virgin rainforest close to beach. Watersports available. 30 minutes drive from Langkawi International Airport.

Golf Club Datai Bay, Jalan Teluk Datai, 07000 Langkawi, Malaysia
T +60 (4) 959 2700, F +60 (4) 959 2216
www.dataigolf.com
18 holes, 6555 yards, par 72, design: Landmarks Berhad

Singapore

Singapore

The Sentosa Resort & Spa
2 Bukit Manis Road, Sentosa, Singapore 099892
T +65 (6) 275 0331, F +65 (6) 275 0228
www.thesentosa.com
167 rooms, 43 suites and 4 villas with own tropical garden and pool. 2 restaurants. Spa offering outdoor and indoor treatments. Tennis. 5 minutes drive to Singapore city.

Sentosa Golf Club, 27 Bukit Manis Road, Sentosa, Singapore 099892
T +65 (6) 275 0022, F +65 (6) 275 0005
www.sentosagolf.com, email: sgc_golf@sentosa.com.sg
Serapong Course: 18 holes, 6990 yards, par 72, design, Ron Fream
Tanjong Course: 18 holes, 7050 yards, par 72, design: Pete Dye

Thailand

Phuket

Banyan Tree Phuket
33 Moo 4, Srisoonthorn Road, Cherngtalay Amphur Talang, Phuket 83110, Thailand
T +66 (76) 324 374, F +66 (76) 324 356
www.banyantree.com
115 villas including 13 ultra-exclusive, newly renovated Spa Pool Villas. 6 restaurants. Banyan Tree Spa, 40 m-lap pool and free-form swimming pool. Located on Bang Tao Bay, 20 minutes from Phuket International Airport.

Laguna Phuket Golf Club, 34 Moo 4 Srisoonthorn Road, Cherngtalay, Thalang Phuket 83110 Thailand
T +66 (76) 324 350, F +66 (76) 324 351
www.laguna-phuket.com, email: golf@lagunaphuket.com
18 holes, 6663 yards, par 71, design: Max Wexler/David Abell

Koh Samui

Bo Phut Resort & Spa
12/12 Moo 1 Bophut, Koh Samui, Surat Thani 84320, Thailand
T +66 (77) 245 777, F +66 (77) 245 776
www.santiburi.com
61 deluxe rooms and villas. 2 restaurants, cocktail lounge. Health & beauty spa, sauna. Fitness center. Diving school, windsurfing. Free transportation to Santiburi Samui Golf course upon request. Located on the island's northern tip, facing the beach of Bo Phut, 10 km from Samui International Airport.

Santiburi Samui Country Club, 12/15 Moo 4, Tambon Maenam, Amphur Koh Samui, Surat Thani 84330, Thailand
T +66 (77) 421 7008, F +66 (77) 421 709
www.santiburi.com, email: infosb@santiburi.com
18 holes, 6879 yards, par 72, design: Pirapon Namatra

Koh Samui

Santiburi Resort
12/12 Moo 1, Tambol Maenam, Amphur, Koh Samui, Surat Thani 84330, Thailand
T +66 (77) 425 0318, F +66 (77) 425 040
www.santiburi.com
12 Equatorial suites, 57 deluxe villas and 2 Santiburi Villas. 2 restaurants, pool bar, garden café, beach bar and lounge. Spa. Watersports. Banquet facilities for up to 112 people. 15 minutes by car from Samui International Airport.

Santiburi Samui Country Club, 12/15 Moo 4, Tambon Maenam, Amphur, Koh Samui, Surat Thani 84330, Thailand
T +66 (77) 421 7008, F +66 (77) 421 709
www.santiburi.com, email: infosb@santiburi.com
18 holes, 6879 yards, par 72, design: Pirapon Namatra

New Zealand

Matauri Bay

Kauri Cliffs Lodge
Matauri Bay Road, Matauri Bay, Northland, New Zealand
T +64 (9) 407 0010, F +64 (9) 407 0061
www.kauricliffs.com
The lodge consists of 11 cottages with 2 guest suites each—22 suites including 16 deluxe units. Every suite with private porch and open fireplace. Dining in the main dining room or on the verandas. Living room, meeting room, card room, small computer room. Spa, infinity pool and tennis courts. Helicopter transfer from Auckland 1 hour.

Kauri Cliffs Golf Course, Matauri Bay Road, Matauri Bay, Northland, New Zealand
www.kauricliffs.com, email: proshop@kauricliffs.com
18 holes, 7119 yards, par 72, design: David Harman GCC, Orlando

Photo Credits

Roland Bauer	One&Only Ocean Club	30	Bo Phut Resort & Spa	Bo Phut Resort & Spa	200
	Stoke Park Club	62	Der Öschberghof	Der Öschberghof	96
	The Grove	66	El Tamarindo	El Tamarindo	36
	Marriott Druids Glen Hotel		Evian Royal Resort	Evian Royal Resort	112
	& Country Club	72	Four Seasons		
	Adare Manor Hotel & Golf Resort	76	Hotels & Resorts	Four Seasons Resort Maui at Wailea	14
	Dromoland Castle	80		Four Seasons Resort Scottsdale	
	The K Club Golf Resort	84		at Troon North	24
	Mount Juliet Conrad	90		Four Seasons Resort Costa Rica	
	Der Öschberghof	96		at Peninsula Papagayo	46
	Schlosshotel Friedrichsruhe	100		Four Seasons Resort Carmelo	54, 215
	Amanjena	146		Four Seasons Resort Provence	
				at Terre Blanche	108, 213
Martin Nicholas Kunz	St. Regis Resort, Monarch Beach	18	GHM Hotels & Resorts	The Andaman	184
	El Tamarindo	36		The Datei	188
	One&Only Palmilla	42	Hotels Constance	Belle Mare Plage The Resort	212
	Oberoi Mena House	152		Lémuria Resort of Praslin	162, 214
	Belle Mare Plage The Resort	156	Kauri Cliffs Lodge	Kauri Cliffs Lodge	208
	The Western Cape Hotel & Spa	166	Llao Llao Resort	Llao Llao Resort	50, 215
	The Sentosa Resort & Spa	192	Marriott Druids Glen	Marriott Druids Glen	
			Hotel & Country Club	Hotel & Country Club	214
Dirk Wilhelmy	Rio Real Golf Hotel	Back cover, 116	Mount Juliet Conrad	Mount Juliet Conrad	213
	Villa Padierna	120	One&Only Resorts	One&Only Ocean Club	Cover, 30, 215
	Kempinski Hotel Bahía Estepona	124		One&Only Palmilla	42, 215
	Denia Marriott La Sella		Palazzo Arzaga Hotel SPA	Palazzo Arzaga Hotel Spa	
	Golf Resort & Spa	128	& Golf Resort	& Golf Resort	104
	Hyatt Regency La Manga	132	Pezula Resort Hotel & Spa	Pezula Resort Hotel & Spa	176
	San Roque Club	136	Santiburi Resort	Santiburi Resort	204
	ArabellaSheraton		Schlosshotel		
	Golf Hotel Son Vida	142	Friedrichsruhe	Schlosshotel Friedrichsruhe	100
			Sentosa Golf Club	Sentosa Golf Club	214
Other photos courtesy			Stoke Park Club	Stoke Park Club	212
			Sun International		
Adare Manor Hotel	Adare Manor Hotel & Golf		Hotels & Resorts	Zimbali Lodge	172
& Golf Resort	Resort	213	The Gleneagles Hotel	The Gleneagles Hotel	58
ArabellaSheraton Hotels	ArabellaSheraton		The Grove	The Grove	212
	Golf Hotel Son Vida	214	The Western		
Banyan Tree			Cape Hotel & Spa	The Western Cape Hotel & Spa	213
Hotels & Resorts	Banyan Tree Bintan	180			
	Banyan Tree Phuket	196			

Editor Martin Nicholas Kunz
Editorial coordination Patrica Massó, Angelika Lerche
Introduction Angelika Lerche
Hotel texts by Angelika Lerche

Layout & Prepress Markus Mutz
Imaging Jan Hausberg
Translations by SAW Communications,
Dr. Sabine A. Werner
English Dr. Suzanne Kirkbright
French Brigitte Villaumié
Spanish Carmen de Miguel
Italian Maria-Letizia Haas

Editorial project by fusion publishing gmbh, stuttgart . los angeles
www.fusion-publishing.com

Published by teNeues Publishing Group

teNeues Publishing Company
16 West 22nd Street, New York, NY 10010, USA
Tel.: 001-212-627-9090, Fax: 001-212-627-9511

teNeues Book Division
Kaistraße 18, 40221 Düsseldorf, Germany
Tel.: 0049-(0)211-994597-0, Fax: 0049-(0)211-994597-40

teNeues Publishing UK Ltd.
P.O. Box 402, West Byfleet, KT14 7ZF, Great Britain
Tel.: 0044-1932-403509, Fax: 0044-1932-403514

teNeues France S.A.R.L.
4, rue de Valence, 75005 Paris, France
Tel.: 0033-1-55766205, Fax: 0033-1-55766419

teNeues Iberica S.L.
Pso. Juan de la Encina, 2-48, Urb. Club de Campo
28700 S.S.R.R., Madrid, Spain
Tel./Fax: 0034-91-6595876

www.teneues.com

© 2005 teNeues Verlag GmbH + Co. KG, Kempen

ISBN-10: 3-8327-9095-4
ISBN-13: 978-3-8327-9059-2

Printed in Italy

Picture and text rights reserved for all countries. No part of this publication may be reproduced in any manner whatsoever.

All rights reserved.
While we strive for utmost precision in every detail, we cannot be held responsible for any inaccuracies, neither for any subsequent loss or damage arising.

Bibliographic information published by Die Deutsche Bibliothek. Die Deutsche Bibliothek lists this publication in the Deutsche Nationalbibliografie; detailed bibliographic data is available in the Internet at http://dnb.ddb.de